THE OLD COUPLE

Poems New & Selected

F. PRATT GREEN

The Old Couple

Poems New & Selected

F. PRATT GREEN

HARRY CHAMBERS/PETERLOO POETS

First published in 1976
by Harry Chambers/Peterloo Poets
8 Cavendish Road, Heaton Mersey, Stockport SK4 3DN, Cheshire

ISBN 0 905291 08 5

Printed in Great Britain by
The Scolar Press Limited, Ilkley, Yorkshire

ACKNOWLEDGEMENTS are due to the editors of *The Listener, Outposts, New Poetry I* (Arts Council), *The Poetry Review, English, The Yorkshire Post, The Countryman, Norfolk Fair,* and *The Hibbert Journal,* in whose pages some of the newer poems first appeared.

"Grandmothers" was broadcast by the B.B.C. (*Northern Poets*).

The three poems marked † in the Contents list first appeared in *This Unlikely Earth* (Hand and Flower Press, 1952).

The thirteen poems marked * in the Contents list first appeared in *The Skating Parson* (The Epworth Press, 1963).

Both of these earlier collections by F. Pratt Green are out of print.

The pencil sketch on the front cover is by Owen Waters.

For my two friends, Peter E. Dunn, poet, and Owen Waters, artist.

CONTENTS

The Old Couple

The old couple in the brand-new bungalow,
Drugged with the milk of municipal kindness,
Fumble their way to bed. Oldness at odds
With newness, they nag each other to show
Nothing is altered, despite the strangeness
Of being divorced in sleep by twin-beds,
Side by side like the Departed, above them
The grass-green of candlewick bedspreads.

In a dead neighbourhood, where it is rare
For hooligans to shout or dogs to bark,
A footfall in the quiet air is crisper
Than home-made bread; and the budgerigar
Bats an eyelid, as sensitive to disturbance
As a distant needle is to an earthquake
In the Great Deep, then balances in sleep.
It is silence keeps the old couple awake.

Too old for loving now, but not for love,
The old couple lie, several feet apart,
Their chesty breathing like a muted duet
On wind instruments, trying to think of
Things to hang on to, such as the tinkle
That a budgerigar makes when it shifts
Its feather weight from one leg to another,
The way, on windy nights, linoleum lifts.

Portrait Of A Stoic

When grief shared the front page of his life
With an emergency meeting of the Directors
And the swarming of his bees, he took the bees,
Went up for the meeting, and buried his wife.

His directors put it down to a cold streak
In his nature, or to investments at stake,
Or an unhappy marriage. Actually, without
Intending to, he had acquired a technique.

How cool can you be? How hard can you get?
But the dust on the brim of his bowler-hat,
And a copy of *The Times* carelessly folded,
Betrayed that in fact he was very much upset.

Not being a clubman, and having few friends,
He took the train as usual to Leatherhead,
His face a mask. Only his bees detected,
In his handling of them, that a life ends

When a wife dies. Tomorrow his bowler-hat
Will be well-brushed, his copy of *The Times*
Folded immaculately. The noble Epictetus
Would not have asked more of him than that.

The Death Of Mussolini

They were not far from the frontier.
Although April was warm to the touch,
His heart was colder than a villa
Shuttered against looting, and rags
Of glory exposed his naked terror.
Hadn't he told Clara he would rather
Put his fortunes into cold storage
Than bury himself, like the Fuehrer,
Beneath the ruins of a blind rage?

But within sight of safety, shouts
And shots ended the dud adventure,
As fifteen partisans, out fishing
In troubled waters, struck it lucky,
Landing without effort or difficulty
The biggest fish of the whole catch.
Il Duce! they yelled, as the bells
Preached revenge among the cypresses,
Promising a pardon to whoever kills.

The place was Dongo. It was a gutter
Killing, in which he had no chance
To strut about, to preserve his image,
Like Bonaparte on the Bellerophon.
They hanged him with a rope of jeers,
Then left him dangling. How a man
Dies, strung up or crucified, won't
Matter all that much. Whether guilty
Or innocent, only our legends count.

Old Men In Libraries

Old men who sleep in libraries,
Waking up with the morning's news
Itching in their eyes,
Know heat from cold, peace from
Nagging, not light from twilight,
Sameness from surprise.

They are the vital eye-witnesses
Nobody wants to hear. In moments
Of lucidity they sense
A conspiracy to stop their mouths,
A refusal, when life is on trial,
To take their evidence.

They fought the wars of history
Men write books about. Now
To them 'contemporary'
Means the cloud of a cataract
On the eye or fire of arthritis
In the hip. Let them be,

These drowning men, to whom a chair
Is something to cling to, until
The weather becomes too rough
And at last they let go. *He died
In the library reading the papers*
Is a desirable epitaph.

A Teenage World

Every evening the elderly used to stroll
Up the High Street to the Town Centre,
Window-shopping. Now it's a teenage world,
Where we walk like aliens without passports,
Hoping to get by. If stared at, we smile
With the defensive bonhomie of the senile.

Out of the corners of our watery eyes
We watch the tight-jeaned youngsters flaunt
Their masculinity in front of girls
Whose cupped breasts arrogantly invite
A doorway petting. Slyly, we think
This was a cup from which we used to drink

When we were young. Milling round, they talk
A foreign language, wear outlandish garb.
A juke box blares. Coffee-bars are alive
With a generation beating its time
To cannibalistic rhythms that defeat
Our stiffening joints and spongy feet.

Why are we strangers to our grandchildren?
Why do they contract out of our lives?
The town clock strikes ten. By midnight
We shall all lie between crumpled sheets,
Too far apart to hear each other weep,
One family beneath the low roof of sleep.

The Victim Died Of Stab Wounds

It was when the novelty of life
Wore off he bought a flick-knife;
And the leather jacket he stole
Because it was a status symbol
That helped him to play it cool,
To prove he was nobody's fool.

Then he ganged up. He was only
Doing what insecure, lonely
Types do, as the psychiatrist
Pointed out. Put to the test,
He had no option but to climb
The ladder of petty crime.

What's more vulnerable than age?
A man counting dough in his dotage,
Before the shop door shuts,
Asks for it. But it takes guts
To grab the loot and scarper
Under the busy nose of a copper.

You don't expect old men to show
Fight, to bellow, to blow
A referee's whistle. It's a life
For a life. The flick-knife
Burns in the sweating palm
Of the hand that means no harm.

It's that simple. As for death,
What is it? You buy a wreath,
Pull down a blind, drink a pint
In memory of some old skinflint,
Then put it out of your mind
Until you next pull down a blind.

A death is a natural thing. A killing
Is a special sort of thing.
The slob had let him down by dying;
He lay there not even trying
To live. The flick-knife stuck
Out of him. What bloody luck!

It's the enormity of the offence
Proves, in a way, its innocence.
Not that this helped him much
Before the Bench. He lost touch
Somehow with himself. Disgrace
Stamped on a magistrate's face

Didn't register. What maybe did
Was the shock of the blood
Trickling slowly into a crack.
If he could, he would have put it back
Into the body. That he never can
Makes him, prematurely, a man.

Sonnets For A New Decade
Or Lil And Merle

The young mechanics who jack up our cars,
And handle grease-guns with the expertise
Of those whose next objective now is Mars,
Have discontented and distracted eyes
That quarrel with the garage clock. At five
They knock off work, and dressed as juke-box stars
Parade the streets that keep the town alive.
I see their faces in the coffee-bars.

The pretty ivy hides them as they slip
Arms around Lil and Merle. But am I hard
In my suspicion they are much more scared
Of women than of cars, and less prepared
To measure up to love's apprenticeship
Than lads who went to school with Abelard?

The lads who went to school with Abelard
Parade the streets that keep the town alive,
A problem generation. Watch them jive
With dead-pan faces as a strolling bard
Croons them a ballad of Byzantium;
Or flock to hear a teenage idol rock
The papal boat, and riot round the clock
If Mother Church turns down an angry thumb.

And Abelard? No dialectic skill
That rocks the crib in which the future sleeps
Can reconcile his warring world. He weeps
For Heloise; and even Merle and Lil,
Whose true romances skip the Modernist,
Envy the girl an Immortal Lover kissed.

16

Envy the girl an Immortal Lover kissed?
It's better to be loved with tragic passion
Than share a schizophrenic scientist
With a reactor! Watch the Age of Fission
Changing its patterns as I change my shirt!
Look how that buddy in a donkey-jacket,
Bull-dozing Lovers' Lane to level dirt,
Startles a blackbird from a hazel thicket!

The pretty ivy hides them, Lil and Merle,
As they adjust a strap and trap a curl,
And sip their coffee. Though sub-intellex
(Which Abelard described the Legate as),
They never jitter. Can it be because
Love is our constant in a world of flux?

'Love is our constant in a world of flux'
Is putting it another way than Freud's,
And lets a God in—post tenebras lux!—
Which obviously is something one avoids.
But bells ring up a critical decade
With Tennysonian charm. A finger-tip
May touch destruction off. Or are we made
To measure up to love's apprenticeship?

The scientist packs up his chromosome;
The young mechanics yawn. But Merle and Lil,
Who wonder what it is attracts the male,
Stare into Outer Space. Misty and pale,
The moon exalts them for a moment, till
There's nothing else to do but to go home.

17

Walking With Father

It was expected of me, between chapel
and dinner, to walk with father.
Walking with father was a Sunday ritual,

like winding clocks, cream with the apple-
pasty, and the dead afternoon
waking to the tinkle of crown-derby

at five precisely. Our shoulders back,
we walked to the gusty promenade
by a golf-course where Sabbath-breakers

enjoyed themselves, by a cinder track
edged with the scented mayweed
where stones could be accidentally kicked.

Enoch walked with God, I with my father,
who talked, as I scanned the sea
for Cunarders, of unspecified sins

I had given up guessing at. Rather
than listen, I filled my lungs,
as I was told, with life-giving ozone,

and day-dreamed. Our walk home took us
by fine houses where ship-owners
dined on salmon, by a small terminus

where trams stood or started with raucous
grindings and exciting sparks.
By now father was joking, poking me

with a gloved finger, pleased (I suspect,
looking back) at having got
my sins off his chest, and we arrived

in high spirits, all present and correct,
he would say, as we pushed open
the smell of dinner. After the grace,

my mother would ask, *How did you enjoy
your walk?* forgetting it was
the same walk, the same father, the same boy.

Grandmothers

My grandmothers McCartney and Billington
ticked in our lives like the two clocks
we were proudest of in our Liverpool home.

The dining-room clock was of black marble,
bold-faced and pilastered, with a loud
tick and an imperiously metallic strike;

but the drawing-room clock was a confection
of whispering wheels in a glass case,
prettily gilded, with a silvery-soft voice.

What a contrast they made, my grandmothers
McCartney and Billington, one too buxom
in black silk, one petite in white lace!

My father's mother had been married thrice;
bossy in a house full of bric-a-brac,
she died, out shopping, at twelve o'clock.

My mother's mother had been married twice;
the beloved relict of a drunken lay-about,
she lived with us, mousily, for ten years,

and stealthily departed after sipping milk
laced with brandy. At times, when I stop
to ask myself what it is makes me tick,

I can hear the two clocks chiming together
in my carcase, detect the McCartney in me
playing at cat with the Billington mouse.

Memory Of Liverpool

We boys went to work by the river-ferry,
The gangways steep when the tide was low,
    Leaning on the wind,
    Dodging the spray,
With the lyver-bird golden in the sky,
And the rubbish blown out of a boy's mind.

We came home at night by the river-ferry,
The gangways flat when the tide was high,
    Staring at serpents
    Of light in the water,
With the lyver-bird leaden in the sky,
And the rubbish blown out of a boy's mind.

On days when the fog foxed the river-ferry
We rushed for the lift to the Low-level,
    Swaying on a strap,
    Mouthing a fag,
With only the draught from a black tunnel
To blow the rubbish out of a boy's mind.

You Can't Teach The Heart Not To Stare

When you are eight, and you are old enough
Not to stare at a cripple, not to look back,
Not to ask loud questions then and there,
We shall take you, they said, to see Jack,
Poor Jack, they said, as they looked where
There was nothing to look at, and their lips
Stopped talking, shutting up like mousetraps
Because I was not old enough, I was there.

So when I was eight, and I was old enough
To feed spiders with flies, to feel fear
Prickle the back of my neck, nobody near,
We must take you, they said, to see Jack,
Poor Jack, they said, but be sure not to stare
At his right hand, if he kisses you forget
Who it is, if he speaks to you answer back
Politely, say it is a fine day or a wet.

The day was fine, with thunder in the air,
As we drove from the door with a whip-crack,
Gee-up, whoa-there! Now you are old enough
We are taking you, they said, to see Jack,
Poor Jack, they said, who sits in a chair
All day, all year, watching her, or asleep
Like a child, no use to her, and bringing
Nothing in, doing nothing to earn his keep.

We walked to a cottage, down a rutted lane
Hedged with holly, wicked with nettles, sure
Of finding him in, they said, because Jack,
Poor Jack, has a sickness nobody can cure,
And whatever you do, they said, don't stare
At his right hand, but if he holds it out
Take it, shake it politely, it won't bite,
And accept nothing, only an apple or pear.

Where sunflowers glared at us over a fence
We are here, they said, stroking my hair
To comfort me, seeing Jack was asleep there
In the doorway, with his head lolling back,
And his right hand, small as a baby's, limp,
Dangling, for a hand is nothing to fear
And more use, they had said, than a stump.
But you can't teach the heart not to stare.

Spastics

Walking home afterwards, I am struck
By the lane's stillness in mid-December,
The muffled elms and ghostly hemlock.

Movement there is. A friendly mongrel
Trots by with loose gait; a wood-pigeon
Panics from a tree. This is rational;

And were the wind to blow its head off
In apple-orchards, scattering branches,
This, too, would be natural enough,

For nature does everything with ease,
Even her worst. It is our humanity
Begets the nightmare children, these

Hostages to the uncontrollable flesh,
Who risk themselves like lovable clowns
On their tight-rope lives with a rash

Courage. Watching, who wouldn't confess
He moves here like a mole in daylight?
Are we not all children of darkness?—

As was Brueghel that day he painted
His group of moronic peg-leg cripples,
Pity not being the effect he wanted.

Waving for the last time, I am shaken
By a wasteful and misdirected anger
Against something which is itself broken.

By The River Yare

Here, beyond the boat-yard,
Where the sailing dinghies
Are put to bed until Easter,
I often come in winter-time
To watch the mallards take off
Noisily, as a wind whistles
In tags of metal and turns
Tarpaulin into thunder-sheets,
And the sad-faced anglers,
Shielded by green umbrellas,
Stare at the whipped waters
Of the slow-moving Yare.
How different it is now—
Now the dead staithes echo
To laughter as loving hands
Repair the ravages of winter,
And the boys, the lucky-ones,
Shout in the sun, shaking a
Sail out, and dinghies take
To water, graceful as swans.

In Memoriam : E.W.T.

Today, hearing of your death, I remember
how we slugged each other with satchels,
your cut lip sealing our friendship; how,
between games of bagatelle we slaughtered
tin soldiers, as flags moved backwards
on the sagging map towards disaster; how
we built sand-castles, and abandoned them
to the invading tide, like tired Romans
called home to defend nearer frontiers; how
we lazed in warm hollows among the sand-
dunes, screened by scratchy marron-grass,
furtively probing each other's defences
until we reached the perimeters of alarm,
and drew back; how life parted us, without
cutting the thread, so that for thirty years
we wrote at Christmas, yet without meeting,
until, time pressing, I crossed your path
(you were standing outside a shop, smiling,
clerically benign); how, paralysed by sadness
I drove on. I cannot believe you are dead.

Keeping In Touch

Keep in touch, you always say,
your good-bye handshake
lacking conviction, your smile
charming but impersonal,
like flags on a royal mile.

We know you will be too busy
to keep in touch, and I
too lazy. As you turn away
you add, *It's been a pleasure
meeting you again, dear boy*.

Keeping in touch isn't easy
for people like us;
yet we are genuinely fond
of each other when we do meet
for snooker, once in a while.

After potting the winning black
you will stack your cue,
saying, without conviction,
*We must meet much more often,
dear boy—keep in touch!*

Backslider

I've seen so many chapels in Wales
Called by Bible names, beautiful names,
With their windows square as honesty,
Rounded as charity, clear as purity,
I thought He must have come back;
But the deacons all walked with a tread
So solemn, I thought He was dead.

Why, I cried, are the holy chapels
Surrounded by spikes and spears,
And never a flower but the dandelion,
Which I love, mind you, and the singing
Oh beautiful singing but lugubrious,
And the deacons all dressed in black
As if He had never come back?

So I passed by the chapels of Wales
Respectfully, mind you, and walked
Where lambs sucked, chaffinches sang,
And lilies of the field were arrayed
Better than Solomon, and the thorn
Flowered, and my heart that had lack
Of Him flowered and put off black.

When I touch my cap to the deacons
They call me by bad names, Bible names,
Such as Backslider, and Son of Belial,
But I go to my own chapel, thank you,
Which has no railings, walls, or windows,
With the singing joyful, and my head
Laughing itself off He isn't dead.

Inheritors

Where Londoners rid themselves of distempers,
And exotic pelicans dry their feathers,
The black inheritors of white empires
Sleep in the sun,
Heedless of Africa and its eruptions;

Or stroll by with a muscular elegance,
Arguing about universities and grants
In sonorous vowels and soft consonants,
Itching to ride
In black limousines to white receptions,

In rapid passage from jungle to jungle,
From tribal dance to political struggle,
From sex tabu to the eternal triangle,
Destined heirs
To what discriminations, what deceptions.

Chinese Restaurant

Since Mister Wong opened *The Lucky Star*
Between the Minster and St. Enoch's Square
The exotic has become our daily fare,
And even Vicars Choral stoop to stare
At unburnt joss-sticks in a porcelain jar,
If, my dear Cantor, that is what they are.

Behind venetian slats of duck-egg blue,
A brass Buddha, and eucalyptus plants,
The Archdeacon orders from a pink menu
Beaten-egg soup, and several Africans,
Enjoying life like playful elephants,
Eat their chop-suey with enormous hands.

Over their heads a tasselled lantern turns
From gold to silver with a silken sound
As bowing Mister Wong, whose brother burns
Cash to buy off the demons, with profound
Non-attachment lodges an English pound
In his deep till, computing what he earns.

He earns our gratitude, or perhaps not,
For setting up his Chinese melting-pot
Here in our gothic city, where he watches
Cantonese waiters glide from serving-hatches,
Like him cosmopolite and polyglot,
Turning silver to gold in all he touches.

Only an imperial dragon shows surprise
As foreign devils catch the savoury pork
With chopsticks, celestials with knife-and-fork;
That nobody bothers if it's right or wise
To scorn the Analects and fraternise
With crude barbarians in a cloud of talk,

Obscuring principles the Ancients made
Politely clear. For vital frontiers fade
When Mister Wong places a piece of jade
In a small alcove next to the same sauce
They serve in snack-bars on the West Parade
In any of the Hundred-and-one-Resorts.

This odd encounter with the coloured races
Causes the Archdeacon seriously to ask
If crossing cultures everywhere produces
Merely the incongruously picturesque,
Not knowing the most perfect time and place is
When Madame Wong sings lieder in the dusk.

Upstreet an aerial cuts the moon in half,
And the warm echo of an international laugh,
Born in Kowloon or Kano, bids us meet
Strangers half-way. Let rice be the staff
Of life, my dear Cantor, noodles a treat!
As late as this, there's nowhere else to eat.

Neither Here Nor There

The removal van at the door,
We are neither here nor there.
This is no unusual state
For those whose feet are often
On the moving stair
Between waking and sleeping,
The shallow and the profound,
The ground and underground.

Removal from here to there,
From a farewell to a welcome,
For an insulated hour
Finds us without a home,
And without any need to fear
A loud knock on the door,
Dry-rot in the floorboards,
Skeletons in the cupboards.

And why should we envy those
Who from baptism to funeral
Live in the same burrow,
Whose one and only removal
Is from ground to underground,
Who never know the release
Of being compelled to commit
Goods and selves to transit?

The removal van at the door,
What we have been and done,
Not been and left undone,
Is neither here nor there.
We shall take the road south
With our slate wiped clean—
Or will our ghosts defeat us
By being first to greet us?

Flitting

They call it a 'flitting' in these parts,
Speaking the dialect of an uncompromising
Truthfulness. 'When will you be flitting?'
They ask, not meaning to stab our hearts.

'We shall be flitting next week,' we say,
Trying not to anticipate the poignancy
Of it, and expecting the matter-of-fact
Rejoinder: 'You'll be wanting a fine day.'

A fine day, certainly, would be fitting;
It would take the edge off our farewells.
'Like as not, you'll be glad to get away;
Quickest is best in dying and flitting!'

That's it! To suffer the week-long smart
Of doing so many things for the last time
Gives our removal south a finality that
Twists a knife in the unadventurous heart.

Night-Driving

This is the moment I have waited for.
I turn the headlights up, relax,
And drive into my own bright corridor.

I enjoy night-driving. It's a relief
Not to have a landscape to look at,
Not to have distance plucking at my sleeve.

Tonight there's no moon to confuse me
With its false magic. I prefer
The headlights' selective efficiency,

The beam that catches the criminal fox,
And the crushed hedgehog, betrayed
By armour, its death an anti-climax.

Above the headlights a scatter of stars
Gives depth to a multi-universe
Only darkness convinces me is ours.

Miles, time, are meaningless. I yawn
Prodigiously. It gets colder. Soon
I shall slow down to listen to the dawn-

Chorus, as Adam must have listened before,
Cast out of paradise, he began
This journey I am taking in my car.

Accident

The crash was so impersonal
it took crushed metal
to prove the human element
fallible and mortal.

What was most incongruous
in the shock of crisis
was that lights change colour
though nothing crosses.

As slowly the shaken town
steadied, disappointed
witnesses of a confrontation
went off unwanted.

The rest was simply routine.
While a posse of police
measured guilt and innocence
without trace of malice,

we swapped names and addresses
for the usual purposes,
thankful it wasn't a case
for coffins and hearses.

The Old Man And The Kite

Looking into the sky
I see three things that fly
a bird a plane a kite
the boy is not in sight

his kite is like a dog
taking a boy for a walk
it pulls out the slack
with an impatient tug

if his kite were a plane
(they call a plane a kite)
he'd fly it to America
and be back home tonight

if his kite were a bird
it would fly out of his hand
and not collapse ridiculously
on the oil-slicked sand

The plane is gaining height
the gull is out of sight
the kite has a broken back
the boy hasn't the knack

Look, the boy's in sight!
It's not a boy, it's a girl!
which only goes to prove
nothing is quite right

for if the girl were a boy
he wouldn't be in tears
and O if I were the boy
I wouldn't be seventy years

I'd be flying my new kite
on a bright windy day
instead of writing a poem
to prove I can still play.

Glider

Letting the rye-grass
tease my neck
I laze on my back
with nothing to do
but to keep an eye
on a solitary glider
using a thermal
to laze in the sky
with no other purpose
beyond giving pleasure
on a summer's day
then sink to earth
and be packed up
and towed away
leaving the vast
unlittered sky
with nothing to do
but to keep an eye
on the Vale of Mowbray.

Humanscape

He had travelled in humanscape
All morning, content to miss
A heron in flight and a rock
With a flowing collar of lace,
So intent had he been watching
Weather in eyes and a season
In the open field of a face.

But as soon as the boy got in
At Chard, with a bag of apples
And a fishing-rod, he returned
To the landscape, the more sad
Beholding there in a glass
Darkly the questioning ghost
Of the son that he never had.

Oystercatchers

You hand-in-hand lovers, invading
their island of gorse and rock
at the sleepy hour of low tide,

stepping so happy-go-luckily
in your laughing summer love
on beds of slippery seaweed,

are you deaf to the hullabaloo
the oystercatchers are making,
their wails of panic protest?

Are you ignorant, you young lovers,
that children must be protected,
theirs today, and yours tomorrow,

that these are cries of a love
never quite free from anxiety,
needing an island to enclose it?

Another Sabbath In The Western Highlands

A hooded crow on the Wee-Free roof
is cleaning his feathers. This is a day
for a short walk in a waterproof.

Out of the rain, psalm-singing Christians
clear their consciences, never posing
the bleak and unanswerable questions.

This is a day for listening to the lark
singing in the leaden sky of a summer
cold as Christmas, for watching the dark

waters of the sea-loch slipping away
from the seaweed, the sea-gulls sailing
in long glissandos. This is a day

of dulled vision. In dripping woodlands
primroses rot and the rhododendrons
shake the rain off with hidden hands.

Listen to the crow croaking his psalm
on the Wee-Free roof! This is a day
when we need religion to keep us warm

in the dark kirk where the People of God
witness, with a compulsive holiness,
to the strength of His arm and His rod.

The Tide Is Out - Polperro

The tide is out. Women too old for love
Dawdle down cobbled streets
Wearing their husbands like a glove.

With the wrong caption in its eye
A sea-gull circles the bone-dry harbour,
Posteresque in a cobalt sky.

Cameras click and churr. But discontent
Blurs the picture. Can it be
For lack of the reflective element,

Of the double image? No fisherman
Preparing his bait, no spectator, sees
Upside-down the motionless swan,

Or himself, shaken. Out-of-focus
In the heat, the town's a mere mirage,
Its history more than half-bogus,

A bore. After a valedictory boom
In teas and trinkets, the snake of cars
Glides to the top of the dark combe.

The tide comes in. Gently it fills
The net-hung harbour, washing its bed
Of the day's assorted ills,

Until the slow dipping of an oar
Ruffles a reflection only tranquillity
Could have given or can restore.

Lament For A Cornish Fishing Village

I turned the corner, saw a Lilliputian lighthouse
standing there like a milk-bottle on a doorstep,
and in the green hollow the pocket-sized harbours
guarded by eccentric rocks, the toy boats, cottages—

and my heart stood still, time stood still, I stayed
days over, and came back, next year, year after year,
believing my love would be my love for ever, never
suspicious, angry when others dispraised her, lazy

with her in the sunny weather, admiring her in all
weathers, walking in her moonlight by reflective water,
closing my eyes to the slow corruption of her character,
how she began to wear cheap jewellery, trade on simple

charms, giggle about her buccaneer ancestry, even
give herself Spanish airs, and sell her favours to all
and sundry, the easy-come-easy-go customers, until
I saw her for what she is: an incorrigible prostitute.

Say, if you like, I and my like are snobs, enjoying
our patronage of the unsophisticated and too innocent
girl, who needs to grow up, to be her age, and find
her own lovers. Isn't this, darlings, a free world?

All the same, I send you my good wishes, most of all
to *White Heather*, *Ocean Gift*, *Hopeful Lad*, and to all
deep-sea fishermen, to the small craft, and small boys
sailing them, and to those vulgarity will never corrupt,

and my undying thanks to the sea-gulls and jackdaws,
to the excitable stone-chats, to cushions of thyme,
tufts of sea-pinks, to stone crop, and to foxgloves
on the inaccessible cliffs, and to the cleansing tides.

The End Of The Season

This October morning
the wind has shifted to its winter quarters,
rolls up the season
and walks on the grave of the winkle-woman.

Dreaming, the town
contemplates its cardboard pavilions,
and a sceptical sun
crosses the palm of the sea with silver.

Above the happidrome
the hands that dropt the beaded curtain
in a room of yawns
shuffle the pack and tell their own fortune.

What fortune is ours
who sit gazing into the crystal morning,
self-absorbed,
uncommunicative, clairvoyant?

Harriet And The Psychiatrist

Harriet had a gift for arranging flowers.
She was the kind of woman who would put
    Barbeton daisies with sprays
    Of echeveria in a brass goblet
In an alcove at the foot of the stairs.

She put flowers everywhere. On the table
Beside the telephone, so that the soul
    Was so ravished by freesias
    With fern in a Chinese bowl,
You forgot the number you wanted to call.

That was before she met the psychiatrist.
He was as dried-up as the dead beech-leaves
    She mixed with chrysanthemums.
    He was shapeless. His sleeves
Were frayed where they rubbed a bony wrist.

Perhaps it took a psychiatrist to explain
Her obsession. But to us it was obvious
    She had to organise. If not
    Carnations with pyracanthus
Berries in a mothei-of-pearl shell, then

Someone like Carl. Not both. As she bent
The silver galvanised netting to her will,
    So that magnolia blossomed
    From a cornucopia, she fell
Into the error of the ruthlessly competent,

And fitting Carl into her delusive dream
Of gracious living (just as she might add
    Privet or aspidistra leaves
    To a rich arrangement of glad-
Ioli and crotalaria), she married him.

To Carl, of course, she was mentally sick.
Once he had freed her from her neurosis
    She no longer compulsively
    Wanted to arrange roses
And nerines in a wrought-iron candlestick.

Dear Harriet! When we last called on her
She was mending, competently, a fraying
    Cuff of Carl's. The only
    Flowers were a few decaying
Marigolds in a most unattractive jar.

The Plastic Begonia

In a world of the phoney
Could anything be phonier
Than this plastic begonia
    In its plastic pot,
Too frightful to be funny?

By 'world of the phoney'
I mean this lurid hell
Of a no-star hotel,
    Whose manageress,
With a flair for the toney,

Thinks nothing is tonier
For a bedside table
Than this imperishable
    And pollenless
Abortion of a begonia,

That shocks my serenity
As I slowly undress
With the crude nakedness
    Of its flashy flesh,
Its sexless obscenity.

What would Michel Begon,
Governor of Santo Domingo,
Say of this thingo
    To Father Plumier,
Flower-loving Franciscan,

Who grew daily holier
Hunting for botanical
Rarities, and of all
     Begonias found
The first, *Rotundifolia*,

By a waterfall; or Bligh
Of the Bounty, cursing
Cabin-boys for not nursing
     B. Machrophylla?
Enraged as the captain, I

Dither, risking pneumonia,
Metaphysically sick
That science doesn't stick
     To space probes, glaring
At this plastic begonia,

Daring myself to seize it,
And with a wild shout
Chuck it clean out
     Of the window; fearing
If I did, it would emit

Such a blood-curdling cry
(Like a Draculan vampire
Perishing in fire),
     That I haven't the guts,
God forgive me, to try.

After Reading A Book On Ferns

for Sir John Betjeman

Say Tabitha lived here with her ferns,
Off the High Street, in a cul-de-sac
Into which heavy lorries would back,
Darkening her raftered room, filling it
With echoing oaths too strange to shock
Lonely Tabitha living with her ferns:
    Adiantum cuneatum gracillimum
    Nephrolepis exaltata hillsii
    Phyllitis scolopendrium crispum.

The sword-fern cascading from the stand
(Her kittens would toy with it until
She tapped them), the hart's-tongue on the sill,
Sturdiest of all, the mist-maidenhair
On the what-not, tremulous and still,
Were ferns to her; to those who understand:
    Nephrolepis exaltata hillsii
    Phyllitis scolopendrium crispum
    Adiantum cuneatum gracillimum.

Say that she found a most subtle joy
In her green world. Quite ignorant of
The sublimations of luckless love,
She lightly dusted them with her breath,
Marvelling how their fronded beauty throve,
Having no need of Latin to enjoy:
    Phyllitis scolopendrium crispum
    Adiantum cuneatum gracillimum
    Nephrolepis exaltata hillsii.

When they laid Tabitha in the ground,
Within sound of mattins and evensong,
They planted over her the hart's-tongue
    (*Phyllitis scolopendrium crispum*)
For its hardness; but the tender ferns
They heartlessly left to perish among
The garbage of a cat-infested ground
    (*Nephrolepis exaltata hillsii*
    Adiantum cuneatum gracillimum).

This, I fear, is a dark universe
For the luckless heart, the tender plant;
But it would be the most godless cant
To refuse to give thanks for the things
That have consoled us for a vain want.
Tabitha, help me to praise in my verse
    Adiantum cuneatum gracillimum
    Nephrolepis exaltata hillsii
    Phyllitis scolopendrium crispum.

Question And Answer

I asked the plum-tree: is there a purpose?
Weighed down by a crop heavy as grief
It answered, 'The purpose is to be a tree.
What other purpose could there be?'
But I watched it sicken of silver-leaf.

I asked the willow-warbler: is there a purpose?
Young innocent in the thorny brake,
It answered, 'The purpose is to be a bird.
What other purpose could there be?'
But I saw no mercy in the eye of the snake.

I asked my blood-brother: is there a purpose?
Busy at his craft in the sun-washed room,
He answered, 'The purpose is to be a man.
What other purpose could there be?'
When they called him to breakfast he did not come.

I asked the Hidden One: is there a purpose?
Dear and doomed in brother and bird and tree,
He answered, 'The purpose is creativity.
What other purpose could there be?
Am I not creating you—and you Me?'

Webs

At the heart of the radial beauty
Of its web, an abominable spider
Squats, alert as a hanging judge,
Clouding for me my image of God.

What upsets me is this conjunction
Of beauty and violence. Near by,
Alas and alas, a cheerful victim
Chills the morning with beatitude.

Were I given discretionary powers
To revise creation, would I expunge
These graduates of the inhumanities,
And, in fairness, carnivorous man?

Thinking myself wiser than Wisdom,
And more loving than God-is-Love,
I struggle to escape from this web
Of compassion I have myself spun.

Cain's Self-Defence

My brother Abel was a blue-eyed boy,
His father's pride, his mother's joy
(A younger son knows all the tricks).
He got the cuddles, I got the kicks.

He chose a leisurely life with sheep,
But I had to dig to earn my keep;
While he rode off to pastures new
I was stuck with the things I grew.

His was the suave, devotional air
(How close to blackmail is a prayer?);
So all his sacrifices ascended;
Mine, too perfunctory, offended.

It was his better-than-thou sniff
Earned him a knife in his midriff,
Proving him, in the event, smarter,
Since I am murderer, he is martyr.

By now, Saint Abel, he prays for me
With the same insufferable piety;
For next to murder, nothing's worse
Than being blessed because you curse.

Despite the fuss, I bear no grudge
Against the High and Mighty Judge,
Who merely gave me an awful wigging
And then confirmed me in my digging,

With various curses, all expected,
And a guarantee I'll be protected.
Supposed to be fugitive for life,
I've settled down and taken a wife.

Doubtless the Supreme Intelligence,
Not being, as I suspected, dense,
Spotted the root of all the trouble:
That I am Cain—and he was Abel.

Humanity Lives By Its Myths

A poem for two voices

Humanity lives by its myths,
Thought Noah, father of the future,
And told no other creature.
> *Shem, Ham, and Japheth*
> *Are kneeling down on Ararat*
> *Praising their Creator.*

How could I save them alive,
Whispered Noah into his sleeve,
Unless I made them believe?
> *Shem, Ham, and Japheth*
> *Are dancing up on Ararat*
> *With their pretty wives.*

The Flood was historical fact,
Frowned Noah, and the world wicked:
But was my theology crooked?
> *Shem, Ham, and Japheth*
> *Are mooning round on Ararat,*
> *Hands in their pockets.*

When our drowning neighbours clawed
Our timbers, I cursed the Flood!
Am I more merciful than God?
> *Shem, Ham, and Japheth*
> *Are very quiet on Ararat*
> *And up to no good.*

How could that loving Saviour
Who made the Ark float
Sponge the rest of the world out?
  Shem, Ham, and Japheth
  Are busy now on Ararat
  Breaking up the boat.

I am the father of unbelief,
Sighed Noah; but I must make sense
Of life. I am Homo Sapiens.
  Shem, Ham, and Japheth
  Are doing research on Ararat
  Into elementary science.

Were we to have no myths
With which to cajole and threaten
Our irresponsible children—
  Shem, Ham, and Japheth
  Are messing about on Ararat
  With a nuclear weapon—

I can foresee, groaned Noah,
There would be no Ark at all
Either for man or for animal.

Shipwreck: A Dream Poem

If the ship sinks, we must swim
To that little promontory of sand
We mariners call the land,

If we can swim; we must wade
Through malarial swamps where flies
Batten on human blood,

If we can wade; we must steal
Food from the suspicious villagers
Where the drums throb,

If we can steal; we must creep
Through thick scrub where a lioness
Licks her playful cub,

If we can creep; we must scale
The snowy peaks of the watershed
With ice-pick and rope;

And if we have none, we must die
Where the breath freezes to death
On the blasphemous lips of hope,

If we can die; we must soar
On angel wings to the pearly gates
With the good and the pure,

If we can soar; we must play
On our harps for ever and aye
Our *Miserere Domine.*

Defeat: A Dream Poem

Sire, when the bugler in the blood
Sounded retreat, we had no choice
But to take cover in this wood.

We were not cowards, sire, but men
Too sick to fight and desperate
To lie between clean sheets again.

No order from your High Command
Had reached us, nothing in the book
Fitted our plight in such a land.

So trapped here in this wood we talk
In whispers as the golden day
Slowly withers upon its stalk.

Already through the trees a cool
Wind strikes at the marrow and rots
The narcissus by the stagnant pool.

Sire, we must wait for night to fall.
When suns wink out and the stars fall
We shall escape—or not at all.

The Next Minute

Sluggishly the water moves to the weir,
    Bearing away the unsullied
    Flowers of the wild cherry
The wind scattered over it somewhere.

This sunny minute, on a film of water
    Dry as my hand, drift
    Nature's excitable children,
Whirligig, water-gnat, and pond-skater;

And in sunless burrows the voles rest,
    Watching a bubble blink
    On a round lid of water,
Or sleep, snout tucked in a warm breast . . .

Then flowers quiver as the water folds
    In falling, antennae wave
    And eyes open, alert to
Whatever it is the next minute holds.

The Limit Of Strain

Had pressures been building up during weeks
Of abnormal rainfall, culminating at last
In a spectacular cloudburst in the hills?
Or had there been a secret flaw, a failure
In the great dam itself to resist pressures?
An error of calculation in a fallible head
Or infallible computor? A routine check
Not made on the site by a foreman or inspector?
We are still guessing. Proof is lacking.

Some witnesses speak of an uneasy silence
Before the great dam burst, before disaster
Struck us like a fatal blow to the heart.
Birds had stopped singing, sheep grazing;
A shudder ran down the spine of the world;
And a priest stood gazing up into the sky
As if he saw visions or was waiting for a voice.
In less time than it takes to say a short Mass
In our four villages there were 300 dead.

Funeral processions are over, the dead buried,
And a disaster fund has met all contingencies.
The official enquiry will be inconclusive:
Proof is lacking; there will be no scapegoats.
Who can be sure, given such imponderables,
What is the limit of strain, the breaking-point?
Or what goes on under complacent surfaces? Or
Whether a slight tremor in terra firma
Heralds the sudden end of all we lived for?

Moving Shadows

Let me take hold of your arm.
An invisible wind blows
from the dark side of the moon
to trouble these bare branches
whose shadows we walk upon.

Who walks on moving shadows
shall be shaken by a fear
paradoxical and profound
and harder to quell than his
who treads treacherous ground.

Do not these shadows write
the equivocal fate of Man,
who, steeling himself to meet
reality, lets illusion
betray his wayfaring feet?

Walking In Winter

Friends, on a winter's walk,
    walking in the early
winter of our age, we enjoy
    the pastel morning's
    frosty transparency,
the crackle of casual talk.

Through the beech-woods we go
    to Polesdon Lacy,
pacing it out in a steady
    rhythm that rations
    energy and breath.
To us winter's death is no

death, but a mature season,
    truthful and bare
and beautiful, promising
    revival in root
    and seed of a life
to be tired of would be treason.

Even so, no need evokes
    an easy intimation
of immortality. We grasp
    at the existential
    moment, this winter's
walk, before the weather breaks.

Backs To The Engine

Sitting with backs to the engine
We are not conscious of the future
Menacing us, of harsh mountain,
Long tunnel, and strange terminus;
Only of a present that diminishes
Into blue distance, where horses
Graze in the paddocks of the sun.

From those who are looking back
Nothing is stolen. So we enjoy
A wholly-quiescent mood, in which
It is not we who move but fields
And horses, and the twelve stations
We cannot stop at, each a stage
On our enforced journey in time.

Hidden from us, the blue diesel
Bears us through autumn orchards
Tolerant of winter, by deserted
Playgrounds where a pensioner sits
Waiting for the dismissal bell.
What disturbs us is not speed
But loss of it, this slackening

Of the landscape. Prematurely
We reach for our luggage. The end
Postpones itself; and we've time
To ponder, before we step out
Under that clouded span of glass,
Whether our arrival presupposes
A fresh directive and departure.

Slackwater Stillness

Even as there is a moment of slackwater
before the strong hands of the tidal swell
slap the stone steps in the secret harbour;

as there is stillness after the tenor bell
ceases to call from the dusty chamber and
the clock formally strikes the expected hour:

death be no more than slackwater stillness
between the grief in voices I shall forget
and the joy in voices I shall remember.

Revelation

When He breaks the Seventh Seal
and the iron hooves are still,
arrows shall sleep in the quiver
and kindness speak through steel;

shrouds shall dance in the sun;
with not a shadow between,
lover lie down with lover
housed by the Three-in-One;

the Lamb and Dove shall prevail
and the Seven Wounds shall heal,
and the light of a man's self
shine through his finger-nail.

HOTSPOTS
ANTIGUA

Written by Polly Thomas
Original photography by Polly Thomas and Dexter Lewis

Published by Thomas Cook Publishing
A division of Thomas Cook Tour Operations Limited.
Company Registration no. 3772199 England
The Thomas Cook Business Park, Unit 9, Coningsby Road,
Peterborough PE3 8SB, United Kingdom
Email: books@thomascook.com, Tel: + 44 (0) 1733 416477
www.thomascookpublishing.com

Produced by Cambridge Publishing Management Limited
Burr Elm Court, Main Street, Caldecote CB23 7NU

ISBN: 978-1-84848-178-7

First edition © 2009 Thomas Cook Publishing
Text © Thomas Cook Publishing
Maps © Thomas Cook Publishing/PCGraphics (UK) Limited

Series Editor: Adam Royal
Production/DTP: Steven Collins

Printed and bound in Spain by GraphyCems

Cover photography © Franco Cogoli/4CR

CONTENTS

WHAT'S IN YOUR GUIDEBOOK?

Independent authors Impartial up-to-date information from our travel experts who meticulously source local knowledge.

Experience Thomas Cook's 165 years in the travel industry and guidebook publishing enriches every word with expertise you can trust.

Travel know-how Thomas Cook has thousands of staff working around the globe, all living and breathing travel.

Editors Travel-publishing professionals, pulling everything together to craft a perfect blend of words, pictures, maps and design.

You, the traveller We deliver a practical, no-nonsense approach to information, geared to how you really use it.

ABOUT THE AUTHOR

Polly Thomas is a freelance writer and editor who first travelled to the Caribbean aged 17. Since then, she has visited most of the islands, and is the author of guidebooks to Jamaica and Trinidad & Tobago, as well as numerous articles on the region. She now lives in Trinidad with her partner and child.

 Nelson's Dockyard

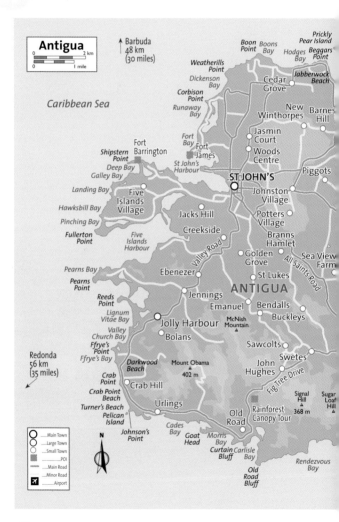

Antigua

| 0 | | | | 2 km |
| 0 | | | 1 mile | |

Barbuda
48 km
(30 miles)

Caribbean Sea

Redonda
56 km
(35 miles)

Prickly
Pear Island
Boon Boons Hodges Beggars
Point Bay Bay Point
Jabberwock
Weatherills Beach
Point
Dickenson
Bay Cedar
Corbison Grove
Point
Runaway New
Bay Winthorpes Barnes
Hill
Fort Jasmin
Bay Fort Court
Shipstern Barrington James Woods
Point Fort Centre
Deep Bay St John's Piggots
Galley Bay Harbour ST JOHN'S
Landing Bay Five Johnston
Islands Village
Hawksbill Bay Village Jacks Hill Potters
Pinching Bay Creekside Village
Fullerton Five Branns
Point Islands Hamlet
Harbour Golden Sea View
Grove Farm
Pearns Bay Ebenezer St Lukes
Pearns ANTIGUA
Point Jennings
Reeds Emanuel Bendalls
Point Buckleys
Lignum McNish
Vitae Bay Mountain
Valley Jolly Harbour Sawcolts
Church Bay Bolans Swetes
Ffrye's John
Point Hughes
Ffrye's Bay Darkwood Mount Obama
Beach 402 m Signal Sugar
Crab Hill Loaf
Point Rainforest 368 m Hill
Crab Point Crab Hill Old Canopy Tour
Beach Urlings Road
Turner's Beach
Pelican Cades
Island Bay Goat Morris
Johnson's Head Bay Curtain Carlisle
Point Bluff Bay
Old
Road Rendezvous
Bluff Bay

⊙	....Main Town
◎	....Large Town
○	....Small Town
■	....POI
	....Main Road
	....Minor Road
✈	....Airport

N

Getting to know Antigua

Sitting at the northern end of the Leeward chain, the twin island nation of Antigua and Barbuda is one of the Caribbean's most popular holiday destinations. Antigua is a tiny, predominantly flat island of just 280 sq km (108 sq miles), measuring only 17 km by 22 km (11 by 14 miles) at its widest points. Lying 48 km (30 miles) to the north, Barbuda is just 160 sq km (62 sq miles) and lies mainly below sea level.

In the 16th century, European settlers arrived and began developing the islands in earnest, turning Antigua into a giant sugar plantation, which by the 18th century was worked by a population of African slaves shipped in by the British. Barbuda served as a market garden, its produce feeding the settlers and slaves over on the larger island. Antigua also became central to British military strategy in the region, since its sheltered harbours proved ideal for the establishment of a naval dockyard. The legacy of the colonial era remains very much in evidence today, first and foremost in the distinctive ruins of the circular cut-stone windmills, which are scattered across the landscape, and also in the traditional red British phone box, the Georgian architecture and place names such as Falmouth, which still lend the island a sense of 'Englishness'. Yet, since gaining independence from Britain in 1981,

REDONDA

Antigua and Barbuda also lays claim to a third piece of territory, the tiny island of Redonda, a barren and uninhabited slab of rock of around 1.6 sq km (½ sq mile), lying 56 km (35 miles) to the southwest of Antigua. Redonda's main claim to fame is the fact that over the years several individuals from various countries have declared themselves 'king' of the island. The current claimant, 'King Robert the Bald', is a Canadian man, Bob Williamson who has reigned since 31st May 1998 and established a consular outpost in 2007 at the Wellington Arms pub in Southampton, England, in an ultimately unsuccessful bid to beat the new smoking ban there.

Antigua and Barbuda have shaped a culture that is very much their own, best expressed in brilliant festivals such as the summer Carnival, when the locals take to the streets dressed in bejewelled and feathered costumes, and in the delicious cuisine, which includes fiery pepperpot stew, cornmeal fungi and sweet-potato *ducunu*.

The pace of life is laid-back, and, though there are some lively bars, clubs and restaurants in the main tourist resorts, Antigua is a quiet place on the whole – Barbuda even more so. Nonetheless, there's a huge amount to do and see within the islands' diminutive dimensions, as the slogan of the tourist board – 'The beach is just the beginning' – might suggest. The glorious beaches are one of Antigua and Barbuda's biggest draws, but, aside from sun and sand, you'll find fascinating colonial history at Betty's Hope sugar estate, Nelson's Dockyard and the crumbling fortifications at Shirley Heights, and plenty of natural allure in the verdant Fig Tree Drive or the mangroves and shallow waters of the North Sound Marine Park.

⬤ *The pristine beach at Half Moon Bay*

THE BEST OF ANTIGUA

TOP 10 ATTRACTIONS

- **Trip to Barbuda** With some truly spectacular deserted beaches and a fascinating frigate bird colony, Barbuda is the ultimate unspoiled Caribbean island (see page 63).

- **Devil's Bridge** Lashed by foaming Atlantic waves, this natural limestone arch is one of Antigua's natural wonders and an essential stop-off (see page 37).

- **Boat cruise** Gentle catamaran cruises around Antigua's coast are a great way to visit secluded beaches and snorkel over some of the island's best reefs (see page 97).

- **Nelson's Dockyard** Built by the British under Lord Nelson, this is the oldest working Georgian dockyard in the world and a fascinating repository of naval history (see page 47).

- **Fig Tree Drive** Bordered by lush tropical foliage and banana plantations, this meandering road through Antigua's interior provides some scenic contrast to the beaches and is home to an exciting canopy tour (see page 84).

- **Shirley Heights Sunday Lime** Experience Antigua's best-known and most popular get-together as the sun goes down over English Harbour. Alongside smoking barbecues, live bands playing steel-pan, reggae and calypso music get the dancing going after dark (see page 80).

- **North Sound Marine Park** Surrounded by teeming reefs and sprinkled with tiny islands that are home to rare plant and animal life, the marine park is best explored by way of an eco-oriented kayak trip (see page 39).

- **Adventure Antigua tours** Whether you go for the 'Xtreme' circumnavigation of the island aboard a powerboat or take a more leisurely eco-trip, this local company offers some of Antigua's best water tours (see page 97).

- **Beaches** With 365 glorious and varied beaches – one for every day of the year – Antigua and Barbuda's seashores are second to none (see pages 24, 33, 43, 57 and 63).

- **Dinner at Papa Zouk** This unpretentious little restaurant in a St John's backstreet cooks up delicious Creole seafood and mixes an excellent rum punch (see page 21).

◗ *Dickenson Bay*

SYMBOLS KEY

The following symbols are used throughout this book:

ⓐ address ☏ telephone ⓕ fax ⓦ website address ⓔ email

🕒 opening times ⓘ important

The following symbols are used on the maps:

𝑖	information office	◯	main town
✉	post office	◯	large town
🛍	shopping	○	small town
✈	airport	▪	POI (point of interest)
✚	hospital	—	main road
🛡	police station	—	minor road
🚌	bus station		
✝	cathedral		

❶ numbers denote featured cafés, restaurants & evening venues
venues in the same area may share the same number

RESTAURANT RATINGS

The restaurants on this guide have been graded with the following symbols, which indicate the price of a three-course meal without drinks:

£ under EC$50   ££ EC$50–100   £££ over EC$100

▶ *Azure waters at Half Moon Bay*

RESORTS
Places under the sun

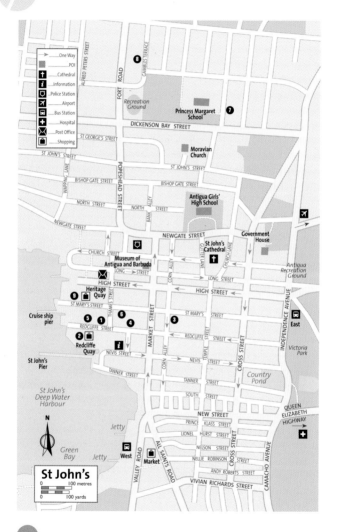

St John's

0 — 100 metres
0 — 100 yards

St John's

Compact and colourful, Antigua's capital offers the most hustle and bustle you'll find anywhere on the island. Spreading back from the sea up a gentle slope, and topped by the towers of the cathedral, its narrow streets are lined with shops and offices, old-time Caribbean wooden façades blending with modern concrete constructions. If you're driving, note that there's a somewhat confusing one-way system in place (which is marked on the map opposite) and that parking on the road is inadvisable. Your best option is to leave your vehicle at the car park between Redcliffe and Heritage quays (accessed from Redcliffe Street) and explore on foot. On days when the huge cruise ships dock adjacent to Heritage Quay, the entire town is overshadowed by their massive bulk and the surrounding area – Redcliffe and Heritage quays in particular – buzzes with music blasting from speaker boxes and crowds piling into the shops and restaurants. If you're after a quieter scene, try to avoid St John's on these days (frequently, but not exclusively, Thursdays and Fridays).

THINGS TO SEE & DO

Antigua Recreation Ground

Just east of the cathedral via Long Street, the nation's hallowed cricket ground – affectionately known simply as the 'Rec' – was the home of cricket in Antigua and Barbuda for many years. It was renowned as one of the best pitches in the Caribbean and was as well known for the infamous party spirit of the 'Double Decker' stand as for the games played. The shiny new Sir Vivian Richards Stadium near Parham was built to replace the Rec in time for the 2007 Cricket World Cup. However, following the cancellation of a West Indies–England Test in February 2009 due to a dangerous playing surface, its future as the island's Test venue seems uncertain, and the Rec may yet return to its former glory days. It still holds a special place in the hearts of West Indian cricket fans as the ground where Viv Richards scored a Test century against England off just 56 balls during the 1986 'Blackwash' series, in which the Windies trounced the English by winning all five games. Brian Lara also notched up 400 not out against the English here in 2004, setting a new record innings for an individual in Test cricket.

ⓐ Corner of Long Street and Independence Avenue

Heritage Quay

Located just north of Redcliffe Quay, across St Mary's Street and adjacent to the cruise ship dock, Heritage Quay is a modern shopping centre. It has less charm than Redcliffe Quay but more in the way of generic duty-free emporia and American-style bars, all designed to service the needs of the passengers who pour in from the ships.

ⓐ St Mary's Street

Museum of Antigua and Barbuda

Set in the grand former courthouse, a Georgian building fronted with neoclassical pillars and arches, Antigua and Barbuda's national museum

🔺 *A cruise ship in dock at St John's*

holds a limited but engaging assortment of exhibits. Although it does not have interactive, state-of-the-art displays, it does give some interesting background on the islands' geology and history, from Amerindian settlement to the plantation era and emancipation. Of the contemporary exhibits, look out for the letter addressed to 'my people' from Britain's Queen Elizabeth II on the occasion of the islands gaining their independence in 1981, and a diorama dedicated to the batsman Sir Vivian Richards, a local man and West Indian cricketing hero.

ⓐ Corner of Long and Market streets ❶ 462 1469
ⓦ www.antiguamuseums.com 🕘 09.00–16.00 Mon–Fri, 09.00–14.00 Sat, closed Sun ❶ Admission charge

Public Market

In a modern building at the southern end of Market Street, the capital's produce market is busiest on Saturday mornings, when trading starts at 05.30 and stalls overflow into the courtyard out front. It's a great place for a browse, with piles of artistically displayed local fruit and vegetables, from prickly green soursops to hot peppers, to enormous pumpkins and tubers of yam and dasheen. In front of the market, the street is dominated by a huge concrete statue of the late V C Bird, so-called 'Father of the Nation'. A giant of local politics, he served as Antigua and Barbuda's first Prime Minister after independence and remained the country's leader until 1994 when, at the age of 84, he handed over the reins to his son Lester. Although many locals speak warmly of the man they called 'Papa Bird', he was a controversial figure, with a reputation for corrupt dealings on a huge scale.

ⓐ Market Street 🕘 06.00–16.00 Mon–Sat, closed Sun

Redcliffe Quay

One of the prettiest and oldest parts of St John's, Redcliffe Quay overlooks the ocean, its shops and restaurants set in restored cut-stone Georgian buildings. They were built by the British during the plantation era, when this was the island's main port. Both sugar and slaves were traded here. Now redeveloped with tourists in mind, its clapboard

⬥ *Statue of V C Bird, St John's market*

frontages fetchingly painted in bright shades, Redcliffe Quay is a lovely place to explore, with some interesting gift shops and some pleasant places to eat and drink.

ⓐ Redcliffe Street

St John's Cathedral

Overlooking St John's from its hilltop position, the twin towers of the Anglican cathedral dominate the skyline. The original wooden church here was built by the British in 1681, under the order of governor Sir Christopher Codrington. It was replaced by a brick building in 1720, which was designated a cathedral in 1842, but a devastating earthquake in 1843 left it in ruins. Today's cathedral was sturdily rebuilt in stone, with its interior encased in dark-stained pitch pine – effectively a building within a building – to strengthen it in the face of another earthquake or hurricane. The gravestones outside carry many memorials to long-departed British planters, while the pillars of the south gates (originally the main entrance) hold statuettes of St John the Divine and John the Baptist, which were taken from a French ship en route to Martinique in 1756 during the Seven Years War.

ⓐ Newgate Street ❶ 462 0820 ● 09.00–17.00 daily, services at 06.15, 08.00, 11.00 & 19.15 on Sun

Victoria Park

Set on a slope, the 2-ha (5-acre) Victoria Park was once a full-blown botanical garden, originally laid out in 1893 by the British. Several handsome trees remain, some of them still with identifying labels, but it's pretty much just a park these days, with a few benches on which to sit in the shade and enjoy the cool breezes coming up from the sea.

ⓐ Independence Avenue and Queen Elizabeth Highway

TAKING A BREAK

Kalabashe £ ❶   Located in the Vendors' Mall, this is a great little diner offering vegetarian food, including Thai-style tofu curry or veggie 'meatballs' in a ginger and honey sauce. The smoothies, especially the fortifying sea moss one, are excellent. ⓐ 10 Vendors' Mall, Redcliffe Street ⓣ 562 6070 ⓛ 08.00–10.00 Mon–Sat, closed Sun

Mama Lolly's Vegetarian Café £ ❷ Tucked into a tiny shop in Redcliffe Quay, with tables outside too, this café serves up delicious and healthy vegetarian food. It also does egg- and wheat-free cakes and fish specials on Tuesdays and Fridays. The juices and smoothies are excellent. Try one blending honey and oats for a healthy boost, or wheatgrass and ginseng for an extra kick. ⓐ Redcliffe Quay, Redcliffe Street ⓣ 562 1552 ⓛ 09.00–17.00 Mon–Sat, closed Sun

Roti King £ ❸ The best place in town – some say the whole island – for roti, a flour-based 'skin' wrapped round curried vegetables and meat, shrimp or conch. The food is cheap, filling and delicious, and you can take away or eat in. ⓐ St Mary's Street ⓣ 462 2328 ⓛ 10.00–01.00 daily

Australian Homemade ££ ❷ This is the place for fabulously decadent home-made ice cream, from macadamia nut crunch to fresh strawberry or mango sorbet. They also sell fine handmade confectionery, waffles and cakes – great for reviving yourself after a hard day's sightseeing. ⓐ Redcliffe Quay, Redcliffe Street ⓣ 462 1941 ⓛ 09.00–21.00 daily

Big Banana – Pizzas in Paradise ££ ❹ This eatery is set over two floors, with a bar downstairs, an outdoor area and an air-conditioned dining room. The menu includes omelettes or pancakes for breakfast, while throughout the day and evening there are salads, burgers, pasta and pizzas with all the classic toppings. Delivery is available, too. ⓐ Redcliffe Street ⓣ 480 6985 ⓦ www.bigbanana-antigua.com ⓛ 08.30–24.00 Mon–Sat, closed Sun

Café Napoleon ££ ❷ With tables on a covered patio in the heart of Redcliffe Quay, this busy French-style café has excellent food, from proper croissants and coffee at breakfast to quiche Lorraine, fresh tuna

Niçoise and filled baguettes at lunch. ⓐ Redcliffe Quay, Redcliffe Street
ⓣ 562 1820 ⓛ 08.30–16.30 Mon–Sat, closed Sun

Commissioner Grill ££ ❺   Located right between Redcliffe and
Heritage quays in a lovely old building, this grill restaurant has a menu
of simple but tasty food including burgers, salads and Creole shrimp.
It's also good for breakfast, serving local specials as well as eggs and
bacon. If you're looking for a drink, there's a bar area, too.
ⓐ Corner of Redcliffe Street and Commissioner Alley ⓣ 462 1883
ⓛ 10.00–23.00 daily

Hemingway's ££ ❻   A lovely setting in a colonial-era building, with
tables in the breezy interior and on a shady balcony. The lunch menu is
light and tasty, with highlights such as conch fritters or steamed cockles.
The dinner menu features shrimp and okra curry and a lovely calypso
chicken breast stuffed with garlic plantain mousse. The service here is
good. Breakfast is available, too. ⓐ St Mary's Street ⓣ 462 2763
ⓦ www.hemingwayantigua.com ⓛ 8.30–23.00 Mon–Sat, closed Sun

Papa Zouk Fish & Rum ££ ❼   One of Antigua's most enjoyable
restaurants, this unpretentious place, tucked away in a backstreet,
serves top-notch Creole seafood, including a 'Carnival Platter' of fish and
shellfish in excellent sauces. The house Ti Punch is tart and delicious and
there are more than 200 rums behind the bar. ⓐ Hilda Davis Drive, off
Dickenson Bay Street ⓣ 464 6044 ⓛ 19.00–late Mon–Sat, closed Sun
ⓘ Book ahead in high season

Home £££ ❽   Here you'll find memorable Caribbean gourmet cooking
in a pleasant setting. Menu highlights include conch salad, fish cakes in
a papaya and pimento sauce, and pork tenderloin in a tamarind sauce.
The guava mousse and coconut crème brûlée make for decadent
desserts. ⓐ Gambles Terrace ⓣ 461 7561
ⓦ www.thehomerestaurant.com ⓛ 19.00–22.00 Mon–Sat,
closed Sun & June–mid Aug ⓘ Book ahead

AFTER DARK

C&C Wine Bar ££ ❷   Genial bar, with tables in a shady courtyard outside, that's popular day and night. Good range of South African wines and light snacks. On Friday nights there are excellent fish dishes provided by Mama Lolly's. They also do other themed food nights. ⓐ Redcliffe Quay, Redcliffe Street ❸ 460 7025 ❹ 10.00–late Mon–Sat, closed Sun

The Coast ££ ❽   The north's busiest and best club, with an indoor, air-conditioned dance floor and an outdoor deck where live bands play on Mondays, Wednesdays, Saturdays and Sundays. The weekends are busiest, when DJs play a mix of reggae, soca, house and dance music. Regular special events are also hosted here. There's a pickup shuttle from many of the island's hotels, but you'll need to organise your own transport home. In addition, the dockside restaurant serves good seafood lunches and dinners. ⓐ Heritage Quay ❸ 562 6278 ⓦ www.coast.ag ❹ Restaurant: 10.00–18.00 Mon, 10.00–23.00 Tues–Sat, 18.00–23.00 Sun; club: 21.00–late daily

King's Casino ££ ❾   Icily air-conditioned casino offering card games (including blackjack and three-card or Texas hold'em poker), roulette and rows of slot machines. Big screens show sporting events and horse racing, and there's live entertainment in the evenings on Fridays, Saturdays and Sundays. ⓐ Heritage Quay ❸ 462 1727 ❹ 10.00–04.00 Mon–Sat, 18.00–04.00 Sun

⬥ *The traditional British phone box – a reminder of Antigua's colonial past*

Dickenson Bay & Runaway Bay

One of Antigua's most tourist-oriented locations, the area around Dickenson Bay is thick with hotels, restaurants and bars, while the bay itself offers one of the liveliest beach scenes on the island. Heading south from Dickenson to Runaway Bay, there are a couple more idyllic sandy beaches that offer more peace and quiet. There's also some historical interest at Fort James, overlooking St John's harbour.

BEACHES

A kilometre (²/₃ mile) of fine golden sand and calm blue waters bordered to the north by the scrubby Weatherills Point and to the south by Corbison Point, **Dickenson Bay** has a very resort-like feel, with a non-stop line of hotels and restaurants lining the beach, sunloungers arranged in rows, and buoys designating swimming areas for the various hotels. There are a couple of great bars right on the sand, making it a nice spot after dark as well as in the daytime, and it's also something of a watersports centre, offering everything from waterskiing and jet-skiing to banana-boat rides, parasailing, snorkelling and diving. For a quieter swim, there's a less developed slip of beach south of the Siboney Beach Club; follow the path beyond The Beach restaurant.

For even more solitude, take the rutted dirt road in between the salt ponds and the sea, beyond Corbison Point, to **Runaway Bay**. Another pristine kilometre (²/₃ mile) of beach, this one is even better than Dickenson Bay, with whiter sand and clearer water – though, as it's practically undeveloped, there is the odd bit of flotsam on the shore. Refreshments are available from the Sandhaven (see page 28) at the southern end of the beach, where customers can also rent jet-skis, sunloungers and umbrellas, and use the showers. Bear in mind that, while the beach is usually deserted, it gets mobbed on cruise ship days, when passengers are bussed in en masse.

Past Runaway Bay, the road swings inland, sprouts some tarmac and then heads back to the coast to **Fort Bay**, another pretty stretch of

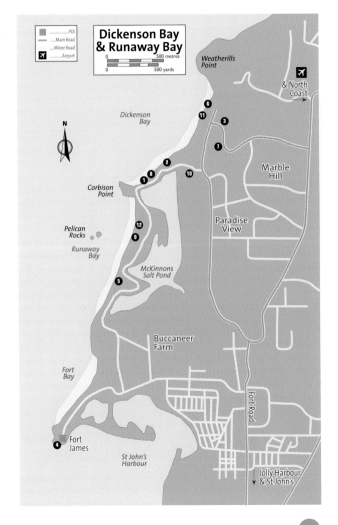

slightly coarser white sand with a little more wave action than its neighbours. Popular with locals, it gets busy at the weekends, with cars parking up in the sandy area behind the beach and families making a day of it. Food and drink are available from Miller's at the northern end.

THINGS TO SEE & DO

Fort James

Built by the British in the early 18th century to stand sentry over St John's harbour, Fort James boasts a commanding position, enclosed by high stone perimeter walls and offering lovely views out to sea and back towards the capital. Although the surrounding lawns are mown, the fort is in a terrible state, with most of its buildings (the powder magazine, the master gunner's house and the mess) ruined and open to the elements, some daubed with graffiti and others the victim of fire. However, this deserted feel somehow adds to the atmosphere of a place whose heyday is long in the past. You can walk freely around to examine the buildings and the ten cannons pointing over the ramparts out to sea and over the harbour.

TAKING A BREAK

Chippy Antigua £ ❶ A local institution, this brilliant little mobile fish and chip van sets up a few tables just off the road adjacent to the Siboney Beach Club. The food is fresh and reasonably priced, with scampi, fish and lobster bites as well as sausage, chips and home-made pies to choose from. ⓐ Dickenson Bay ❶ 724 1166 ❶ 16.00–21.00 Wed & Fri, closed Sat–Tues & Thur

The Beach ££ ❷ A lovely waterside restaurant, with tables on the sand and in a covered open-sided dining area. The menu includes pizzas, pasta, burgers, salads and sushi, and there's a tempting range of desserts, including chocolate soufflé and an apple and rum bread pudding. It's a lively place for a drink and a DJ gets the dancing going on

◆ *On the defensive at Fort James*

a Friday, when the bar sometimes stays open later. Free wi-fi access is available here. ⓐ Dickenson Bay ⓣ 480 6940 ⓛ 08.30–24.00 daily

Pari's Pizza ££ ❸   A Dickenson Bay institution and good for families, this eatery is set above the bay and has a distinctive indoor waterfall backlit in green – there's a whiff of the 1970s in terms of décor. They serve inexpensive and tasty pizza, as well as some pasta and steak dishes. The service is friendly, with takeaway available, too.
ⓐ Dickenson Bay ⓣ 462 1501 ⓛ 17.30–23.30 Tues–Sun, closed Mon

Russell's ££ ❹   Occupying a lovely colonial-era house in historic Fort James, this is a laid-back and elegant place, with live jazz at the weekend (particularly worth catching on a Sunday) and an appetising menu of Caribbean staples including local cockles, spiced red snapper and lobster, cooked up with a twist. It also has a well-stocked bar and good views over the beach. ⓐ Fort James, Fort Bay ⓣ 462 5479 ⓛ 12.00–22.00 Mon–Sat, 16.00–23.00 Sun

Sandhaven ££ ❺   This simple little beach hotel is a good bet for lunch or dinner, with a choice of salads, burgers, fajitas, seafood and mains such as Thai curry or chicken in a white wine sauce. Its bar, overlooking the bay, is also good for a drink or sundowner (there's a pool table and a two-for-one happy hour 18.00–19.00 daily). Sunday is their family-friendly day, Wednesday is film night, and there are various DJ sessions and open-mic nights. ⓐ Runaway Bay ⓣ 771 6803 ⓛ 08.00–late daily

Warri Pier ££ ❻   The location is the main draw here, with the restaurant sitting on a pier built out into Dickenson Bay. The candlelight and the lights of the hotels on the hill twinkling in the distance add a romantic touch. Menu highlights include the smoked salmon and mango tart and the grilled aubergine and courgette lasagne. A full range of seafood is also on offer. ⓐ Halcyon Cove hotel, Dickenson Bay ⓣ 462 0256 ⓛ 18.30–22.00 Mon–Sat, closed Sun

◆ *Pristine sand and crystal-clear water at Runaway Bay*

Bay Gardens ££–£££ A lovely setting on a terrace above the bay with views down to the sea, this hotel restaurant offers all-day breakfasts – including English and Antiguan versions – as well as excellent lunches, featuring pasta, salad, wraps, rotis and burgers. It also has some tasty and varied dishes on the dinner menu. The Moroccan spiced kingfish comes highly recommended. ⓐ Trade Winds Hotel, Dickenson Bay ⓣ 462 1223 ⓦ www.twhantigua.com ⓛ 07.00–23.00 daily

Coconut Grove ££–£££ ⓫ This delightful little thatched restaurant right by the water's edge offers breakfast, lunch and dinner daily. It is a popular drinking spot, too. The cooking is consistently good, particularly at dinner, with such delights as crab tartare, crab bisque, calamari, lobster, snapper with sweet potato, or rack of lamb with orange tamarind sauce. The mango cheesecake and coconut pie are memorable desserts. ⓐ Dickenson Bay ⓣ 462 1538 ⓦ www.coconutgroveantigua.net ⓛ 07.30–23.00 daily

La Bussola £££ ⓭ With a beautiful setting in an elegant open-sided dining room and beachfront garden next to the sea, this friendly place offers excellent Italian cooking and great service. Highlights from their award-winning chef include the saltimbocca (veal in a white wine sauce, layered with prosciutto and mozzarella), the mahimahi in filo pastry and the tiramisu. ⓐ Runaway Bay ⓣ 562 1545 ⓦ http://labussolarestaurant.net ⓛ 10.00–24.00 daily

AFTER DARK

Tattooz £ ⓮ Popular English-run spot, worth a look for a drink any night of the week (happy hour 18.00–19.00 daily). DJs play a wide variety of music on Wednesdays and at the weekends. Inexpensive food (curries, pizzas and burgers) is also available, and there's a mini-golf course to keep the children entertained. ⓐ Dickenson Bay ⓣ 463 4653 ⓛ 16.00–late Mon–Thur, 14.00–late Fri–Sun

◆ *Dickenson Bay is excellent for watersports enthusiasts*

Tony's Watersports £ Right on the beach, this is a laid-back locally run joint, with pool tables, speakers broadcasting reggae music and a mean rum punch served at the bar. Local food is also on offer, including barbecue chicken and ribs, salad and soup. ⓐ Dickenson Bay ⓣ 462 6326 ⓦ www.tonyswatersports.ipage.ag ⓛ 08.00–late daily

Rush ££ Just past Dickenson Bay, this indoor air-conditioned entertainment complex includes Conor's sports bar (a good spot for watching sporting events on the big screen), Madison's casino (with slot machines and card games) and the Rush nightclub, which has a Latin night on Wednesday, live music on a Thursday, party nights on Fridays and Saturdays, and drinks promotions on Sundays and Tuesdays. ⓐ Old Runaway Bay ⓣ 562 7874 ⓛ 22.30–late daily

Long Bay & the east

Antigua's east is nothing if not diverse, with quiet pastures and tiny villages interrupted by areas of tourist development, such as at Long Bay, and both a wild Atlantic coastline of limestone rocks and wave-washed sand and placid, shallow beaches surrounded by reefs. There's plenty to occupy your time away from the beach, too, from the atmospheric ruins at Betty's Hope, once a thriving sugar plantation, to lunch at the beautifully situated Harmony Hall restaurant, followed by a browse around the art gallery there. If you want to get up close and personal with the area's marine life, you can explore the waters of the North Sound Marine Park.

BEACHES

Although Antigua's east is bordered by the rough and wind-blown Atlantic Ocean rather than the placid Caribbean, there are still some splendid beaches. Most are fairly rugged, but of the calm spots the best is **Long Bay**, just north of **Indian Town Point** and **Devil's Bridge**. This is one of the island's most beautiful beaches – a lengthy strip of whiter-than-white sand lapped by clear, shallow waters – and there's a teeming reef just offshore that promises great snorkelling. To cap it off, the constant trade winds blowing in off the Atlantic mean it never feels too hot. There are a couple of all-inclusive hotels here, but non-guests are free to enjoy the beach, with lots of locals coming to swim alongside the visitors. The shallow waters make it especially good for children. You'll find vendors selling sarongs and crafts and the Life's a Beach shop selling drinks and renting sunloungers, umbrellas and jet-skis. Bear in mind, though, that the sand can get crowded on cruise ship days, when throngs of passengers are bussed in.

At the other end of the scale, **Half Moon Bay** is an undeveloped (save for what's left of a hotel that closed down after damage by Hurricane Luis in 1995) and ravishingly beautiful beach – a wide crescent of fine, soft white sand licked by Atlantic waves and a cooling sea breeze. The

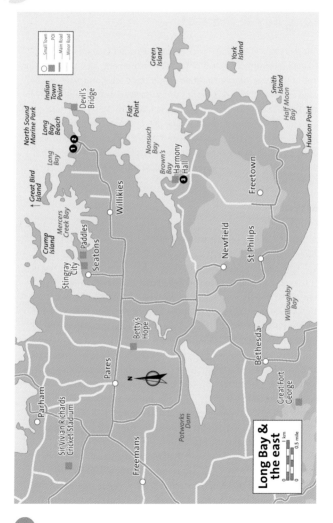

Long Bay & the east

turquoise waters make for an invigorating swim, and, best of all, you'll often have the whole swathe entirely to yourself. To get here, follow the road along the north side of Willoughby Bay, a gorgeous route through dry, scrubby forest, punctuated by cacti and the odd abandoned windmill. There are frequent heart-stopping views down to the blue waters of the bay below. As it climbs above Willoughby Bay, the road forks; the right-hand turning leads to the Crossroads Centre, built by Eric Clapton as a treatment centre for recovering addicts; the left fork takes you to Half Moon. There are no facilities on the beach, but on the access road you'll find Smiling Harry's bar, which has soft drinks and beers.

THINGS TO SEE & DO

Betty's Hope

Betty's Hope is a former sugar plantation that has been transformed into a museum dedicated to Antigua's plantation era, when massive sugar-cane estates owned by the British were worked by slave labour. Established in 1650, Betty's Hope was the island's first plantation, and was owned and operated continuously by the Codrington family from 1674 until 1944, when they sold it to the state. It fell into disrepair and, in 1987, work began to restore and conserve the site. Much of it remains in ruins, and the place has a desolate and deserted feel today, with the sun-bleached bricks of the boiling house and manager's house overgrown with weeds. There's usually a guide on hand to give you a little of the estate's history, which is also detailed in the exhibitions at the visitor centre in the former cotton storeroom. There's a model of the plantation in its heyday, a collection of implements salvaged from the fields, photographs of the restoration process and background information on sugar-cane production and slavery in Antigua.

Perhaps the most impressive buildings are the two windmills, standing tall over the flat plains of the north as you enter the site. One of these has been fully restored, with its sails reinstated and the iron machinery inside that was used to crush the cane repaired.

ⓐ Pares ⓣ 462 1469 ⓛ 09.00–16.00 daily ❶ Admission charge

⬥ *One of two carefully restored windmills at Betty's Hope*

Devil's Bridge

Antigua's remote eastern tip feels a world away from the pretty resort beaches of the west. It is a wild and weather-beaten slab of jagged, potholed limestone, pounded by the constant trade winds and Atlantic waves that, with no land between here and Africa, have some 5,000 km (3,000 miles) to build up momentum. This powerful wave action has eroded the soft limestone to form Devil's Bridge, a natural arch over the frothing, churning water below. It's said to have been named during the plantation era, when legions of slaves committed suicide by throwing themselves into the waters rather than endure the horrific conditions on the estates. Locals came to believe that the devil himself must inhabit an area where so many people died. Waves periodically splash up in the gap between the bridge and the mainland, spitting spray high into the air and ensuring that only the very foolhardy would attempt to cross. To do so would also risk damaging the fragile rock.

Designated part of the **Indian Town National Park** in the 1950s, the promontory that holds the bridge provides protection for a rocky and undeveloped beach to the north, overlooked by a tall century plant (the national plant). Beyond the next promontory lie the calm waters and white sands of the popular **Long Bay** (see page 33). To get to the bridge, take the potholed road signposted for the Verandah Resort (driving east, it's the first road to the right past the entrance to the Emerald Cove gated community) and turn left where the road forks; watch out, as the road surface is very poor. Keep going until the road runs out and the sea is visible.

ⓐ Indian Town Point

Harmony Hall

Set in one of the loveliest locations on the island, in sheltered **Brown's Bay** and with views out to **Nonsuch Bay**, this cut-stone plantation house and sugar mill now operates as a luxurious hotel and restaurant (see page 42). In 2007, the complex changed hands and the new owners established an exclusive yacht club here; in season plenty of masts – including those of the club's own fleet of Dragon racing yachts – bob in

⬙ *Crashing waves at Devil's Bridge*

the waters below. If you're not a yachtie, there's still plenty to enjoy. Lunch guests can use the swimming pool and beach, or alternatively take a boat ride to the privately owned Green Island, where there are great beaches and snorkelling.

Harmony Hall also houses an art gallery, which has regular exhibitions of paintings, sculpture and pottery by Antigua-based artists and a good gift shop. For refreshment, the Sugar Mill bar is open all day. Bear in mind, though, that it is a bit of a trek to reach. From the main coast road, you take the road for Half Moon Bay, and from there turn off onto a rutted and badly potholed road – it's easily drivable in a regular car, but expect a bumpy ride. Book ahead for both lunch (served from 12.00 to 15.00) and dinner (served on Friday and Saturday only).

ⓐ Brown's Bay, near Freetown ☎ 460 4120
ⓦ www.harmonyhallantigua.com 🕒 09.00–18.00 daily (early Nov to mid-May), plus 18.00–21.00 Fri & Sat
❶ Charge for Green Island trip; book ahead

North Sound Marine Park

Just offshore from the tiny fishing village of Seatons, the North Sound Marine Park is a diverse ecosystem of shallow waters and reefs that harbours a huge array of creatures, from turtles and stingrays to brightly coloured shoals of fish. The mangrove-fringed islands are home to a variety of bird and animal life, from red-billed tropicbirds and frigate birds to fallow deer and the Antiguan racer snake (thankfully a harmless variety), which lives only on Great Bird Island. The best way to experience the park is to take a tour with **Adventure Antigua** (see page 97) or **Paddles**, just east of Stingray City in Seatons (follow the signs). Their half-day excursion starts with a boat ride to a lagoon, where you transfer to kayaks and paddle around the mangroves, with guides explaining the area's ecosystem as you go. You then motor to uninhabited Great Bird Island, where you take a guided walk and can swim off one of the two white-sand beaches or snorkel over the reef. Paddles make two trips daily, and can provide transportation to and from your hotel; the tour price includes snorkelling equipment and refreshments. You should wear

◓ *North Sound Marine Park*

swimming gear under your clothes, and bring plenty of suncream, mosquito repellent and something dry to change into.
ⓐ Seatons ☎ 463 1944 Ⓦ www.antiguapaddles.com ❶ Tour fee; book ahead

Stingray City

Set in the village of Seatons, with its fine views out to sea and over to the numerous islets of the North Sound Marine Park, Stingray City might seem like a strange idea for a tourist attraction, given the general perception of rays as dangerous creatures. In fact, Caribbean stingrays are incapable of wilfully using their barbed spines to attack, and only employ them as a reflex defence mechanism when stepped on. As the guides here will tell you, they're actually pretty intelligent and curious, and are happy to be handled and fed by the stream of visitors who take the short boat ride from the base out into the ocean to the shallow sandbar where Stingray City is located. You can don snorkelling gear and swim with the rays or snorkel over the reefs; guides are on hand to take pictures of you interacting with the rays. Trips leave four times daily, and you should arrive 15 minutes before departure time. You'll need swimwear, a towel and dry clothes.

ⓐ Seatons ☎ 562 7297 🅦 www.stingraycityantigua.com 🕒 Trips leave at 09.00, 11.00, 13.00 & 15.00 daily ❶ Admission charge

TAKING A BREAK

Mama Pasta £ ❶ Up on the hill above Long Bay, with tables under a thatched roof, this cute little locally run place offers big plates of inexpensive and tasty pasta, some good fish dishes and local specialities.

🔺 *A solitary mobile café at Devil's Bridge*

It makes a good lunch stop, if spending the day on the beach.
ⓐ Long Bay ⓣ 722 5503 ⓛ 10.00–15.00 Mon & Wed–Sun, closed Tues

The Beach House ££ ❷   This is a great spot with tables overlooking the water from a beachside terrace. The menu is simple but tasty, including several salads, sandwiches, a refreshing chilled 'soup of the day' and more substantial dishes, such as sautéed grouper, pasta primavera and sirloin steak. It hosts a beach barbecue with a steel band every Thursday evening. ⓐ Long Bay Beach Hotel, Indian Town ⓣ 770 9659 or 463 2005 ⓦ www.longbayhotel.com ⓛ 10.30–22.30 daily ❶ Book ahead on Thur

Harmony Hall £££ ❸   A romantic venue for lunch or dinner, with tables laid out on a terrace, offering views of the bay below. The sophisticated menu is a delicious mix of Italian and Caribbean cuisine, with highlights such as marinated wahoo salad, tuna carpaccio and grilled steak. Excellent wine list, too. ⓐ Brown's Bay ⓣ 460 4120 ⓦ www.harmonyhallantigua.com ⓛ 09.00–18.00 daily (early Nov to mid-May), plus 18.00–21.00 Fri & Sat

Falmouth & English Harbour

The hub of Antigua and Barbuda's yachting scene, Falmouth and English Harbour are dedicated to all things nautical, with several marinas, where crafts of all sizes can moor up, and a host of businesses – from chandleries to sailmakers – devoted to the needs of yachtsmen. The area is very much tied to the calendar of regattas and boat shows staged here: visit when one is taking place and you'll find the bars and restaurants buzzing and the marinas bristling with masts. At other times – particularly during the summer, when many businesses shut up shop for a few months – it can feel like something of a ghost town, with only a handful of places to eat and drink and the beaches largely deserted.

Driving into the area from the west or east, you'll come first to Falmouth Harbour, a wide but sheltered anchorage and one of Antigua's oldest harbours. There are a few restaurants and bars here, but the majority of the tourist infrastructure is concentrated in English Harbour, site of the historic Nelson's Dockyard. This is the only working Georgian dockyard in the world, now a national park and with an excellent museum and plenty of buildings to explore. Above the dockyard to the southeast looms the bulk of Shirley Heights (see page 79).

BEACHES

One of the most popular places for a swim in the English Harbour area is **Pigeon Beach**, on the other side of the peninsula from Nelson's Dockyard and facing onto Falmouth Harbour. To get there, carry on along the potholed road past the Antigua Yacht Club Marina, and bear right at the two forks in the road. It is a long swathe of white sand, with clear waters, good snorkelling and a busy beachside restaurant, Bumpkin's (see page 52). It can get crowded during peak season, so if you're after some more seclusion, you could ask one of the boat taxis that moor at the Antigua Yacht Club Marina to take you to **Rendezvous Bay**, the next bay to the west from Falmouth Harbour. A secluded and stunning beach with clear

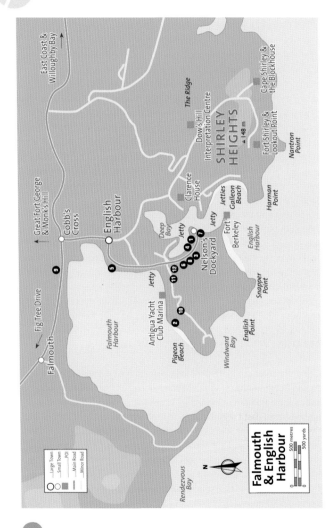

Falmouth & English Harbour

waters and absolutely no development, it's backed by dry scrub and palm trees, and is otherwise reachable only by a 40-minute hike. The lovely **Galleon Beach** (see page 80) is on the eastern shore of English Harbour opposite Fort Berkeley and reachable via the road to Shirley Heights.

THINGS TO SEE & DO

English Harbour

At the eastern end of Falmouth, the road swings south at Cobb's Cross towards English Harbour, a loosely defined area that encompasses the eastern shore of Falmouth Harbour as well as English Harbour itself, and is separated from Falmouth by the promontory that gives the waters of Nelson's Dockyard their protection. The access road and the road to the dockyard are lined with restaurants, bars and shops, and in peak season and during the many regattas and boat shows staged in the area this is one of the liveliest parts of the island. Slightly away from most of the action but very much part of English Harbour nonetheless, the Antigua Yacht Club Marina extends out into the waters of Falmouth Harbour and is home to bars, restaurants and an excellent bookshop.

Falmouth Harbour

With three marinas jutting out into the water – the Catamaran, Antigua Yacht Club and Falmouth Harbour jetties – the wide sweep of Falmouth Harbour is very much a hangout of the yachting community. There's a tiny slip of beach adjacent to the Catamaran Hotel, but it's not particularly impressive, and, as most of the area's restaurants and bars are over at English Harbour, the majority of visitors who spend time in Falmouth do so because they've arrived by boat.

Great Fort George

One of Antigua's oldest forts, having been built in 1689 by the British as part of their system of defences to protect Falmouth Harbour from invasion by the French, Great Fort George is spread over some 3 hectares (8 acres) and served as a signal station and stronghold for valuables,

● *Roof supports for the ruined sail loft, Nelson's Dockyard*

women and children. There's not much left today, with the crumbling ruins of the water cisterns, powder magazine and cannon emplacements overgrown with vines and trees, but its position overlooking the bay from the top of Monk's Hill offers really spectacular views of Falmouth and English Harbour. To get to the fort, take the Mamora Bay turnoff from the main road, which runs around the bay at Cobb's Cross, then take the immediate left. The road is pretty rough and only navigable in a four-wheel-drive vehicle, and even then you'll have to walk the last steep stretch to reach the lofty perimeter walls.

② Monk's Hill

Nelson's Dockyard

Antigua's main historic site and one of its most popular tourist attractions, the restored Georgian buildings of Nelson's Dockyard were constructed by the British in around 1725. British Navy warships, which patrolled the waters of the Eastern Caribbean, defending colonial territories from the constant threat of attack from the French and other European powers, were maintained here. The British brought in African slaves to work in the dockyard, and, at its peak, more than 300 men worked here. Of the officers who presided over them, the most famous is Horatio Nelson, who arrived in 1784 and left in 1787. Reputedly, he didn't like Antigua at all, writing that he was 'most woefully pinched' by mosquitoes and calling the island an 'infernal hole'.

Although the dockyard was oversubscribed during the continuous skirmishes of the 18th century, the defeat of the French at the Battle of Waterloo in 1815 led to the end of hostilities in the Caribbean, and thereafter the dockyard slowly fell into decline. It was abandoned by the Navy in 1889. Handed to the colonial government in 1906, it was subsequently hit by several hurricanes, causing major structural damage. Restoration began in earnest when the buildings were fixed up and readied to cater to the needs of yachts rather than warships.

Now a national park, it is as much a heritage tourism site as it is a working dockyard and marina. At the entrance to the complex, where there's a craft market, a bank and a post office, there's a National Parks

◓ *Copper and Lumber Store Hotel, Nelson's Dockyard*

office where you pay your fee and are assigned a guide who gives you a short tour of the dockyard before leaving you to explore independently.
ⓐ English Harbour ⓣ 481 5022 ⓛ 08.00–18.00 daily ⓘ Admission charge, which also covers entry to Shirley Heights (see page 79)

Admiral's Inn Built between 1785 and 1788 out of stone brought over from England, the Admiral's Inn commands a prime position at the entrance to the dockyard, and now houses a hotel and restaurant (see page 51). Under the British, its ground floor was used to store pitch, lead and turpentine, while the rooms upstairs – now converted into hotel accommodation – served as offices for dockyard engineers. It's a lovely place for a meal or drink, with part of the bar made from a dockyard workshop worktop, the names of boats carved into the wood. The outdoor terrace, meanwhile, has lovely views over the twin rows of stone pillars, which are all that remains of a huge boathouse and sail loft.
ⓐ Nelson's Dockyard ⓣ 460 1027 ⓦ www.admiralsantigua.com
ⓛ 07.00–21.30 daily

Copper and Lumber Store and Officers' Quarters Beyond the Dockyard Museum (see page 51) is the Copper and Lumber Store Hotel, a fine stone building with shuttered windows and swathes of bougainvillea against its walls. The inside boasts a lovely sunlit courtyard. The adjacent two-storey Officers' Quarters is the largest structure in the dockyard, with a grand staircase leading to the upstairs rooms – now converted into shops and a restaurant – which were built over 12 water cisterns with the capacity for 1,200 tonnes of water. Behind the building, the stone quayside has mooring points for the hosts of yachts that dock here during the regattas. On the other side, the dockyard is littered with maritime memorabilia, including three huge capstans, used to haul down ships' masts, and the massive Camelford Anchor, weighing in at 3,200 kg (7,000 lbs) and said to sit on the spot where in 1797 one Lieutenant Lord Camelford shot Lieutenant Peterson during an argument over seniority.
ⓐ Nelson's Dockyard ⓣ 460 1160

◆ *Galleon Bay, English Harbour*

Dockyard Museum Housed in a pretty wooden building dating from 1855 that was built as an officer's residence with handsome verandas both upstairs and down, the museum's displays provide comprehensive coverage of the dockyard's history. There's also a section on British military history in the Caribbean and, upstairs, another on Nelson that includes a bed said to have belonged to him (though he never actually slept in it). Other highlights include the finely detailed model ships and the collection of trophies from the various regattas held here.
ⓐ Nelson's Dockyard ❶ 481 5022

Fort Berkeley Built between 1704 and 1745 to defend the site of Nelson's Dockyard, Fort Berkeley sits at the end of the thin strip of land that encloses English Harbour. It originally had 29 cannons, though only one remains, pointing out to sea through the circular cannon battery right at the end of the peninsula, from where there are lovely views across to Galleon Beach (see page 80). There's also a restored powder magazine, built in 1811 to hold 300 barrels of gunpowder, and a guardhouse from the original construction. The trail to Fort Berkeley winds along the cliffside from behind the Copper and Lumber Store; it's about ten minutes' walk from the dockyard.

TAKING A BREAK

More than other places on the island, restaurants and bars in Falmouth and English Harbour operate seasonally, with many closing up during the slow summer months and outside of the regatta season. Closing times are included below, but bear in mind that these vary a lot year to year; the **Antigua Nice** website (ⓦ www.antiguanice.com) has listings of opening hours, which are updated annually.

Admiral's Inn ££ ❶ Occupying a prime position overlooking Nelson's Dockyard, this place makes an atmospheric spot for a meal, be it on the shady terrace or in the historic interior. The mainly Caribbean menu includes Creole shrimp, 'catch of the day' and lobster salad, but there are

also club sandwiches and soups. ⓐ Nelson's Dockyard ☏ 460 1027
🕐 07.30–22.30 daily

Bumpkin's ££ ❷   A beach restaurant offering tables on a covered
veranda right on the sand and a simple but tasty menu of salads, burgers,
chips, fresh fish, lobster and shrimp. The bar mixes up a good rum punch
and frozen fruit smoothies, and the beers are always ice cold. ⓐ Pigeon
Beach, Falmouth Harbour ☏ 562 2522 🕐 08.00–19.00 daily

Cloggy's ££ ❸   Busy Dutch-run café adjoining Abracadabra (see page
56), with seating on a breezy gallery or in the garden, and a wide range
of well-prepared lunches, such as chicken satay or goat's cheese salad
with grilled chicken and pesto, as well as sandwiches and smoothies, ice
cream and sorbets. It does great coffee, too. ⓐ Dockyard Drive, English
Harbour ☏ 463 8083 🕐 10.00–16.00 Mon–Sat, closed Sun & low season

Life ££ ❹   Occupying a deck over the water close to the entrance to
Nelson's Dockyard, this is a lovely place to grab a drink or meal. Friday is
curry night, with a wide selection of north Indian favourites including
chicken tikka, tarka daal and lamb rogan josh. There's also a traditional
English Sunday lunch, seafood and burgers. In the evenings there are
concerts and screenings of big sporting events and movies.
ⓐ Dockyard Drive, English Harbour ☏ 562 2353 🕐 11.00–15.00 &
17.00–late Tues–Sun, closed Mon

Pasta Rite Ya ££ ❺   Italian-run restaurant with its own dinghy dock on
Falmouth Harbour (hence popular with yachties). Made fresh on site, the
pasta is delicious and reasonably priced, and there's also 'catch of the
day' or fillet steak served with dauphinoise potatoes. Good wine list and
excellent coffee. ⓐ Dockyard Drive, English Harbour ☏ 764 2819
🕐 11.00–24.00 Mon–Sat, closed Sun & low season

Le Cap Horn & Pizza Oven ££–£££ ❻   One of English Harbour's best
restaurants, serving fine French-inspired cuisine, such as Parmesan-

◆ *Yachts, catamarans and frigate birds in English Harbour*

crusted rack of lamb with rosemary jus and scallops sautéed in white wine. The puddings are as spectacular as the main courses – try the bitter chocolate cake with caramelised pineapple. The adjoining pizzeria turns out 12 different pizzas, baked in a wood-burning stove.
ⓐ Dockyard Drive, English Harbour ① 460 1194 ① 18.00–22.00 Mon–Wed & Fri–Sun (pizzeria opens until 23.00), closed Thur & low season

HQ ££–£££ ❼ A fantastic setting upstairs in the Officers' Mess, this elegant restaurant offers authentic French cuisine, including dishes such as foie gras, duck confit and escargots. The lunch menu features salad niçoise, pizzas and burgers. It's a pleasant evening hangout, with regular live music and a jam session on Sunday evenings. ⓐ Nelson's Dockyard ① 562 2563 ① 12.00–15.00 & 18.30–22.00 daily, closed low season

🔺 *A rusting anchor at Galleon Bay, English Harbour*

AFTER DARK

The Gallery ££ ❽   This is an eternally popular place on the road between Falmouth Harbour and the Dockyard. It has a meaty menu, which includes steaks, excellent burgers, good seafood and salads. The tapas also make a great accompaniment to drinks. The dance floor hots up after 22.00 in season, with dance and house music on the decks. ⓐ Dockyard Drive, English Harbour ❶ 562 5678 ⓛ 18.30–late daily, plus 12.00–15.00 Sun (peak season); 18.00–late Wed–Sun, closed Mon & Tues (low season)

Havanna ££ ❾   This is a Cuban-style bar and restaurant in the courtyard of the Anchorage Centre, on the approach road to the dockyard. It is a good spot for mohitos, caipirinhas or tequila shots. There's regular live music and a menu of reasonably priced steaks, grilled fish and chicken. ⓐ Dockyard Drive, English Harbour ❶ 788 4342 ⓛ 18.00–late Mon–Sat, dinner served until 22.00, closed Sun & low season

Kesari ££ ❾   For something a little different, try the Asian tapas here – from wild ginger and sweet shrimp salad to duck and spring onion soup. Sushi, sashimi and Thai or north Indian curries are also on the menu. The bar specialises in Martinis, with over 30 Martini-based cocktails on offer alongside other cocktail favourites. ⓐ Falmouth Harbour ❶ 460 1361 ⓛ 19.00–late Tues–Sat, closed Sun, Mon & low season

Last Lemming ££ ❿   A lovely location on a raised deck overlooking Falmouth Harbour, this is a great spot for lunch or dinner. However, the main draw here is Sunday brunch, when they serve Eggs Benedict Copenhagen (with smoked salmon instead of ham) and an excellent Bloody Mary. It's a popular place for a drink, with a daily happy hour (16.30–18.30) and live music on Tuesday nights. ⓐ Yacht Club Road, Falmouth Harbour ❶ 460 6910 ⓛ 11.00–late daily, closed low season

Mad Mongoose ££ Falmouth Harbour's main party venue, jammed in peak season with hard-drinking yachties, this is a friendly and fun bar with regular special events, including live music on Friday nights. Happy hour is from 16.00–19.00. The menu runs from 'catch of the day' to steak pie or Moroccan-seasoned lamb shanks. The puddings are good, too. ⓐ Yacht Club Road, Falmouth Harbour ⓣ 463 7900 ⓛ Restaurant: 11.00–15.00 & 18.30–22.00 daily; bar: 11.00–late daily, closed Tues–Thur low season

Trappas ££ ⑫ Ever popular with tourists, expats and locals, this bustling place offers a great combination of swift service and reliable, tasty food at very reasonable prices. The wide-ranging menu includes smoked salmon, Thai fish cakes, curries, Aberdeen Angus burgers and fresh fish. ⓐ Dockyard Drive, English Harbour ⓣ 562 2534 ⓛ 18.00–22.00 Tues–Sat, closed Sun & Mon ❶ Book ahead

Abracadabra £££ ❸ This restaurant serves perhaps the finest Italian food in the area. The fresh pasta dishes, such as pumpkin ravioli with sage, are delicious. The roast suckling pig is also excellent, as are the rich desserts, including a very indulgent cheesecake. 'Abras' is the area's best place for a dance, with lots of special events. There's also a pleasant garden chill-out area. ⓐ Dockyard Drive, English Harbour ⓣ 460 2701 ⓦ www.theabracadabra.com ⓛ 10.00–16.00 & 19.00–late daily, closed low season

Jolly Harbour

A resort development set amid the otherwise quiet west coast, Jolly Harbour comprises a marina and associated shops and restaurants, as well as a casino and golf course. Its spectacular beach is just one of the seemingly endless swathes of postcard-perfect white sand and aquamarine waters that characterise the west coast. Several of these beaches have great little waterside restaurants and views of Montserrat and its smoking volcano on a clear day. Most of the people who spend time at Jolly Harbour are either guests at the area's two hotels or owners of the holiday homes – complete with private boat dock – built right on the water's edge. And with more houses on the way courtesy of a couple of large-scale developments, the area looks set to get even busier.

BEACHES

Home to the busiest beach in the area, Jolly Harbour is very much a tourist enclave. To get to the sand, you have to drive (or walk) past the shopping complex and rows of waterfront condos. Since much of the beachfront is taken up with the two big resorts, it can seem a bit difficult to actually get to the sea. Parking adjacent to the Castaway's restaurant (see page 59) brings you to a lovely portion of beach, with calm, clear waters and powdery white sand. You are able to rent sunloungers and umbrellas here.

Working south along the coast from Jolly Harbour, the next beach of note is **Ffrye's Beach**, far quieter than Jolly Harbour but with the same white sand and crystal-clear waters. The right-hand turnoff for the beach is marked by a pillar and overlooked by a ruined sugar mill; the beach is also the location of Dennis's restaurant (see page 59).

About 100 m (110 yds) or so beyond the turnoff, the road meets the sea at the spectacular **Darkwood Bay**, a fine expanse of white sand with a lively reef, shady parking and a pleasant little beach restaurant and bar, which serves tasty local food. The only drawback is that the road runs parallel to the sand. You will find more of the same at **Crab Hill** and

RESORTS

⬢ *Turner's Beach*

Turner's beaches, with loungers, sunshades and snorkelling gear available from Turner's restaurant (see page 61). There's also excellent snorkelling to be found around **Johnson's Point**, which caps Turner's Beach to the south.

THINGS TO SEE & DO

Mount Obama

Inland of Turner's and Crab Hill beaches and rising up from the neat rows of spiky pineapple plants that make up the 8-hectare (20-acre) Cades plantation, the hill that was formerly known as Boggy Peak is Antigua's highest point, though at just 402 m (1,320 ft), it's not exactly shrouded in cloud cover. It's most notable for the fact that, in January 2009, Antiguan Prime Minister Baldwin Spencer renamed it Mount Obama in honour of the newly inaugurated US President. If you have a 4x4, you can drive almost to the top by following the dirt road that leads inland through the pineapple fields.

TAKING A BREAK

Castaway's ££ Right on the beach, with tables on a cavernous shady deck, this is a good beach bar, offering the usual burgers and seafood – grilled mahimahi, coconut shrimp, garlic lobster – as well as sandwiches and salads in the daytime. Evenings see occasional themed nights. This is a pleasant place for a drink, too, with its daily happy hour from 16.30 to 18.30. The sunset views are fabulous, but the service can be a bit patchy. ⓐ Jolly Harbour Beach ⓣ 562 4445 ⓛ 08.00–22.00 daily

Dennis's ££ In a fantastic setting at the top of a hillock above Ffrye's Bay, this is a great place to sample Antiguan food, such as saltfish, chop-up, curried goat and Creole fish. They also have steaks, pork chops, chicken dishes and roast suckling pig on Sundays. The bar serves up excellent rum cocktails. ⓐ Ffrye's Beach ⓣ 728 5086 ⓛ 11.00–late Tues–Sun, closed Mon

● *The near-deserted beach at Darkwood Bay*

Melini's ££ With tables overlooking the marina, this reliable Italian restaurant serves excellent pasta and stone-baked pizzas, as well as steaks, fresh fish dishes and daily specials. Takeaway available. Service is swift. ⓐ Jolly Harbour Marina ① 562 4173 ⓛ 11.00–22.30 Mon–Fri, 18.00–22.00 Sat & Sun

Turner's ££ This excellent locally run beach restaurant with a friendly, laid-back atmosphere serves simple, fresh food, including crab cakes, lobster salad, curried conch and baby back ribs. The tables sit on a covered porch at the sand's edge. The service is good, and the bar does a nice line in frosty drinks. ⓐ Turner's Beach ① 462 9133 ⓛ 08.00–21.00 daily

Sheer £££ Often touted as the island's best restaurant, Sheer certainly has one of the loveliest locations, with six very private little gazebos connected by wooden walkways ranged down the cliff overlooking Ffrye's Bay. The cooking is special, too, with imaginative use of local ingredients and some unusual combinations in the pan-Asian/South American menu. There's only room for 24 people, so book ahead. ⓐ Cocobay resort, Valley Church beach ① 562 2400 ⓦ www.cocobayresort.com ⓛ 18.30–22.30 Tues–Sat, closed Sun & Mon ❶ Book ahead; smart dress required

AFTER DARK

Dogwatch Tavern ££ Convivial pub and restaurant on the marina, with a good menu, that includes Stilton burgers, steak and seafood. There's a lively scene at the bar, which is popular with long-time visitors to the area. It has a pool table and a dartboard. ⓐ Jolly Harbour Marina ⓛ 18.00–23.00 Mon–Fri, 17.00–23.00 Sat & Sun

◐ *White Bay, Barbuda*

Barbuda

Measuring 24 km (15 miles) from north to south and 12 km (8 miles) from east to west, and with a total area of just 160 sq km (62 sq miles), tiny Barbuda is the ultimate unspoiled Caribbean island, a magical place ringed by truly ravishing beaches, sprinkled with pockets of pink sand and lapped by the Atlantic to the east and the calm Caribbean to the west. Its human population of around 1,500 live in the tiny village of Codrington, and are outnumbered by the 2,500-odd frigate birds, whose nesting colony on the island is one of the largest in the world. A boat trip out to see their nesting sites is one of Barbuda's main draws. With just two hotels, Barbuda is truly untainted by mass tourism, somewhere to revel in the gloriously empty, undeveloped beaches and enjoy the slow pace of life.

BEACHES

Surrounded by reefs, crystal-clear waters and spectacular swathes of whiter-than-white sand, Barbuda's beaches count as some of the very best in the Caribbean. Incredibly, they almost always feel deserted, despite locals gathering at the beach for get-togethers at the weekend, and boats of day-trippers from Antigua descending for a couple of hours several days a week. The Atlantic shoreline to the east is rougher and great for beachcombing, with plenty of shells and coral fragments. The reefs create some calm spots, but take local advice before swimming as currents can be strong. The west coast's Caribbean beaches are best for swimming, and, to the southwest, fragments of crushed shell tinge the sand with swathes of pink. As the beaches have no facilities, you'll need to bring water and refreshments with you. Stretching for an eye-popping 16 km (10 miles), **Palm Beach** is lined by the lagoon on the inland side and is a gorgeous – though shadeless – spot. Working southeast, there's more of the same (but with some shade) at **Palmetto Point** and **White Bay**. In the extreme southeast, **Spanish Point** is the site of extensive reefs and numerous shipwrecks, and offers excellent snorkelling. You can rent

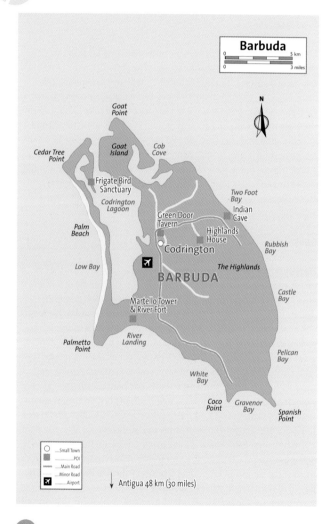

Barbuda

0 — 5 km
0 — 3 miles

N

Goat Point
Goat Island
Cob Cove
Cedar Tree Point
Frigate Bird Sanctuary
Codrington Lagoon
Two Foot Bay
Indian Cave
Green Door Tavern
Highlands House
Palm Beach
Codrington
Rubbish Bay
Low Bay
The Highlands
BARBUDA
Castle Bay
Martello Tower & River Fort
Palmetto Point
River Landing
Pelican Bay
White Bay
Coco Point
Gravenor Bay
Spanish Point

○ ....Small Town
■ ....POI
━━ ....Main Road
── ....Minor Road
✈ ....Airport

↓ Antigua 48 km (30 miles)

gear at the Green Door Tavern in Codrington, which also has sunfish boats and Hobie Cats.

THINGS TO SEE & DO

Codrington
Barbuda's only settlement and the island's capital, Codrington is a tiny little place bordered by the waters of the lagoon to the west. Its name comes from the Codrington family, settlers from Barbados who, in 1685, leased the island for 50 years in exchange for 'one fat sheep on demand'. Subsequent leases were granted up to 1870, and the family came to dominate life here, growing food crops and trawling the wrecks around Barbuda's reefs. Today, Codrington remains an extremely quiet place, with a network of narrow streets lined with neat residences and a handful of businesses. The ambitiously named **Madison Square** holds **Burton's Depot**, the sole supermarket, and the **Green Door Tavern**.

Codrington Lagoon and Frigate Bird Sanctuary
West of Codrington and stretching almost the entire length of the west coast, the shallow waters of the Codrington Lagoon are the main breeding ground for lobsters, Barbuda's second-largest export (after sand, mined for construction use). The roots of the mangrove thickets that predominate here provide perfect protection for young fish and lobsters, and, to the north of the lagoon, the trees also support a huge breeding colony of magnificent frigate birds, which migrate here from the Galapagos Islands to breed. During the mating season (September–April), males inflate a bright red throat pouch to attract females. Once mating has taken place, the birds build a precarious nest in the mangroves and the female lays one egg, which hatches around seven weeks later. Boat tours to see the colony get within about 6 m (20 ft) of the nesting sites, allowing you to view the birds up close and get a whiff of the pungent regurgitated fish that the fledglings feed on. The colony is included in day trips to the island; otherwise, you can charter a boat from the pier at Codrington village.

GETTING TO & AROUND BARBUDA

Barbuda is 48 km (30 miles) north of Antigua. The quickest way to get there is the 20-minute flight with **Winair** (📞 462 2522 🌐 www.fly-winair.com), which has daily flights from V C Bird Airport to the small airstrip just outside Codrington. A cheaper alternative is the **Barbuda Express** ferry (📞 560 7989 🌐 www.antiguaferries.com), which runs on Monday, Tuesday, Thursday, Friday and Saturday, departing from St John's. The journey time is 90 minutes. Most people visit the island for the day as part of an organised tour, one of the best being run by **Tropical Adventures** (📞 480 1225 🌐 www.tropicalad.com) aboard the fast *Excellence* catamaran. The tour includes a boat trip on the lagoon to the frigate bird sanctuary, as well as lunch, a cruise along the coast and swimming at one of the beaches. It leaves from Redcliffe Quay and makes pickups at Dickenson Bay as well. Barbuda Express also runs tours of the island, which include the frigate bird sanctuary, a taxi tour and a lobster lunch. If you don't take an organised tour, you could see the island by hopping in one of the taxis that congregate at the airport and boat dock. Byron Askie, who is the owner of the **Green Door Tavern** (see page 68) and a mine of information on all things concerning Barbuda, also organises island tours.

Highlands House

Northeast of Codrington, a dirt road threads inland towards the Highlands, the only portion of raised ground on an island where most of the land lies below sea level. The highest point is around 40 m (130 ft). The Codrington family chose this appropriately lofty spot to build their home, originally an extensive dwelling, but now reduced to just a few retaining walls and scraps of staircase. Nonetheless, the site affords good views over the rest of Barbuda.

⬥ *Frigate birds outnumber the island's human population*

Indian Cave

Carrying on along the road to Highlands, you'll eventually reach Two Foot Bay, where the rough Atlantic waters are bordered by a rocky shoreline that holds a small cave complex. Once used by Amerindians, who left some petroglyphs – two very faint faces – just inside the entrance, the caves consist of three chambers, two of which are large enough to enter. A ruined building, built by phosphate miners in the 1890s, marks the entrance to the caves.

River Fort

South of the lagoon and presiding over Barbuda's south coast, River Fort is so named because of what is in fact a stream that appears only after heavy rain. It was built in 1710 to defend the island's main anchorage – the adjacent wharf is still in regular use today. Although the original fort was quite extensive, it is now in ruins, and only its thick perimeter walls and Martello tower have survived intact. The tower was one of many that were constructed by the British throughout the Empire during the Napoleonic Wars.

TAKING A BREAK

Green Door Tavern £ A Barbuda institution, this busy place serves breakfast, lunch and dinner, and is the island's long-standing evening hotspot, with speakers blasting out music at the weekends. The food is firmly local, from conch soup or lobster to fresh fish or even Barbudan deer. It's also a great place for a beer or rum. ⓐ Madison Square, Codrington ☏ 460 0065 🕐 07.00–late daily

🜂 *Curtain Bluff Beach*

EXCURSIONS
Out & about

Five Islands

Immediately southwest of St John's, the Five Islands peninsula makes for an interesting excursion after exploring the capital, with some good beaches and lovely views from the lofty stronghold of Fort Barrington. Contrary to what you might expect, there are no sizeable offshore islands here; the area takes its name from five small rocky outcrops. To get to Five Islands, take the road heading west from St John's just south of the market, skirting the south side of the harbour and passing the Multi-Purpose Cultural Centre. At the large roundabout, the right turn takes you to Fort Barrington and Deep Bay, the left (effectively straight on) through Five Islands Village to Hawksbill Bay.

> **GETTING AROUND**
> As Antigua's bus routes are restricted to the main roads, all of the excursions described here are best done by taxi or in a rented car.

THINGS TO SEE & DO

Fort Barrington

The most northerly point of the peninsula is also one of the least accessible. Past the roundabout, the road forks at the entrance to the Grand Royal Antiguan Beach Resort, which sits on the beautiful Deep Bay. Although all beaches in Antigua are public, it's hard to get to this one as the hotel owns the only access road. The right fork at the hotel heads towards the Hideaway Bay condo development. At the sign, take the very rough dirt road – just about driveable in a regular car – that threads through the low scrub to the sea. Cross the rickety metal bridge over the inlet, and follow the path up the hill to reach Fort Barrington, a semicircular construction built in 1779 by the British Admiral Samuel Barrington as part of the defence system for St John's harbour.

◯ *The defences at Fort Barrington*

The 20-minute hike to the top is strenuous, but you're rewarded with fabulous views down over Deep Bay.

Hawksbill Bay

Retrace your route back to the roundabout and turn right, passing rolling fields grazed by horses and cattle, and thread through Five Islands Village. The road soon heads uphill; stop close to the two stone pillars that mark the entrance to the Hawksbill resort for some lovely views over Galley Bay and Hawksbill Bay, the latter named after the offshore rock here that bears a striking resemblance to a hawksbill turtle's head. Just before the resort, you can park at the Royal Palm Beach Park, where there's a lovely strip of beach. Day passes are available if you would like to use the hotel facilities. There are more beaches beyond the hotel, but again accessing them can be tricky, as the only way to do so is by walking through the grounds.

The north coast

Antigua's north is an odd mix, with plenty of hotels lining the coast around Hodges Bay, just west of the V C Bird International Airport – itself now a destination in its own right since the construction of the Stanford Cricket Ground. This place is worth seeing for the fantastic surrounding landscaping alone.

THINGS TO SEE & DO

Hodges Bay

Northeast of Dickenson Bay, Hodges Bay is notable for its upmarket residences and the **Sunsail Club Colonna** hotel (see page 110), from where you can go sailing, with the strong trade winds that blow in off the northeast coast creating excellent conditions for it. Watersports passes that cover sailing, windsurfing and canoeing are available from the hotel, which sits on a decent slip of beach. You can take sailing lessons here, too.

Jabberwock Beach

A handsome swathe of fine white sand, Jabberwock is more a place for watersports than it is for lounging in the sun – it is the island's kitesurfing hotspot. The prevailing winds are best between December and May and in July and August, but whenever there's a breeze you'll find **Kitesurf Antigua**'s trailer set up on the beach, offering lessons and equipment rental. Even if you don't have a go yourself, the acrobatics of the surfers are fun to watch. The conditions are also excellent for windsurfing, and you can rent gear and get tuition from **Windsurf Antigua**, which also sets up on the beach whenever the conditions are right for it.

Kitesurf Antigua ☎ 720 5483 Ⓦ www.kitesurfantigua.com
Windsurf Antigua ☎ 461 9463 Ⓦ www.windsurfantigua.net

◆ *Commemorating the nation's favourite sport at the Stanford Cricket Ground*

Prickly Pear Island

Just off the shore of Hodges Bay and reachable by a five-minute boat ride, Prickly Pear Island is a tiny uninhabited spit of land with a lovely reef-ringed beach. You can visit it as part of the day tours offered by **Miguel's Holiday Adventure**, which include a lobster, fish and chicken lunch and an open bar, as well as snorkelling equipment and use of beach loungers and umbrellas. Trips leave on Tuesdays, Thursdays and Saturdays.

🕿 460 9978 Ⓦ www.pricklypearisland.com ❶ Tour fee

Stanford Cricket Ground

Detour off the road at the airport turning and you might well think you've been transported to a different country. The manicured lawns, landscaped tropical gardens and pastel-painted buildings in faux-Georgian style that make up this area come courtesy of Texan billionaire Sir Allen Stanford. He staged several high-purse Twenty20 matches at the state-of-the-art cricket ground that he built here before being accused of fraud on a massive scale (an alleged Ponzi scheme) in February 2009. It's a surreal scene that's more reminiscent of a Miami theme park than anything Antiguan. However, following the collapse of the Stanford empire, the future of the area and of the company's various buildings (which include a couple of fancy restaurants) is far from certain. Other than perusing the greens of Stanford's cherished cricket ground, you might also want to check out the Cricket Hall of Fame outside the Sticky Wicket bar and restaurant (see below), with bronze sculptures and short biographies of the game's great West Indian players. Otherwise, the 21-m (70-ft) observation tower (🕓 10.00–22.00 daily) affords some lovely views over northeast Antigua and out to the offshore islands.

TAKING A BREAK

Sticky Wicket ££ Within a stone's throw of the airport and with tables overlooking Stanford Cricket Ground, this bar and restaurant is good for a meal or drink even if you're not about to jump on a plane. The very

◆ *The Sticky Wicket, Stanford Cricket Ground*

international menu features light snacks such as calamari, quesadillas, salads, sandwiches, wraps and burgers as well as generous main courses, from herb-roasted half chicken to steaks. The ginger crème brûlée is also pretty good. The icily air-conditioned bar area is bedecked with cricket memorabilia. ⓐ 1 Pavilion Drive, Coolidge ⓣ 481 7000 ⓦ www.thestickywicket.com ⓛ 11.00–23.00 daily

Le Bistro £££ One of Antigua's more upmarket restaurants, offering modern French cuisine and attentive service. The extensive menu features everything from duck breast salad to snails in garlic butter, trio of lobster, mahimahi and snapper in a basil sauce. Expensive, but deservedly so. ⓐ Hodges Bay ⓣ 462 3881 ⓛ 19.00–24.00 Tues–Sun, closed Mon

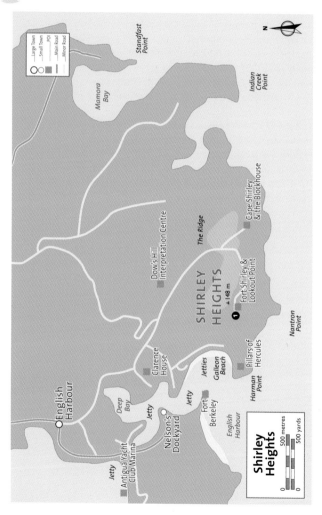

Shirley Heights

Looming over English Harbour, Shirley Heights is named after General Thomas Shirley, governor of the British Leeward Islands between 1781 and 1791, who fortified the hillside during a stint in Antigua to protect Nelson's Dockyard below – crucial in maintaining the military might of the British Navy in the Caribbean. Today, the scrubby, sun-parched hillside is dotted with the remains of Shirley's fortifications, some of which have been restored. There are also several well-marked hiking trails; maps are available from the National Park office at Nelson's Dockyard (see page 47). Shirley Heights is also the site of the island's most enduring party, the Sunday Sunset Lime (see page 80).

ⓐ Shirley Heights, English Harbour ☎ 481 5021 ◷ 09.00–17.00 daily
ⓘ Admission charge (included in ticket to Nelson's Dockyard)

THINGS TO SEE & DO

The following attractions can be followed as a tour, starting on the road coming from English Harbour.

Dow's Hill Interpretation Centre

About halfway up the hill, there's a booth at the side of the road where you pay your entrance fee (or show your ticket if you've already paid at Nelson's Dockyard). Just off the road here, behind the ruined Dow's Hill fort, the Interpretation Centre has an ambitiously named multimedia exhibition, 'Reflections of the Sun', in which a voiceover gives a rather pedestrian history of Antigua.

ⓐ Shirley Heights ☎ 481 5045 ◷ 09.00–17.00 daily

Cape Shirley and the Blockhouse

At the very top of Shirley Heights – keep straight on along the main road – Cape Shirley is a barren and windblown spot that affords some spectacular views over the southeast coast to Mamora and Willoughby bays. Look out for the house ranged over the cliffs at Standfast Point,

a promontory to the east – it belongs to rock star Eric Clapton. On a clear day, Montserrat and Guadeloupe are also visible. The buildings here are known collectively as the Blockhouse; most are ruined, though a couple – such as the boxy guardhouse – have been painstakingly restored over the years.

Lookout Point

Heading back down the main road, take the left-hand fork to reach Lookout Point, the most heavily visited part of Shirley Heights as the site of the Sunday party. The restaurant itself occupies a handsome former guardhouse, and outside there are fabulous views back down over the dockyard and English Harbour. It is also a great place to catch the sunset. On the approach to the restaurant, the ruined Officers' Quarters, with their crumbling arches, make for some atmospheric photographs.

> **SHIRLEY HEIGHTS SUNDAY SUNSET LIME**
> Each Sunday, the restaurant at Shirley Heights (see page 82) is Antigua's place to be, when seemingly half the island descends for the outdoor lime (the Caribbean parlance for a get-together). From 16.00 a steel band plays as the sun sinks over English Harbour (one of the best sunset views on the island). From 19.00 the barbecue doles out sizzling burgers and a local band plays reggae and calypso tunes. With everyone dancing and the rum punch flowing, the party atmosphere develops. It's an enjoyable event, popular with tourists and locals, and fine for families as well. There's a quieter version each Thursday, with a steel band from 16.00 to 20.00.

Galleon Beach

Along another (signposted) left-hand turn just before you get to the bottom of the hill, Galleon Beach boasts a gorgeous swathe of fine yellow sand and clear waters, with stunning views over to Fort Berkeley.

◗ View from the Shirley Heights Lookout

Adjacent to the dinghy dock, a huge rusting anchor sits half-buried in the sand; it was once used by sailing ships to winch themselves into the harbour. There are a couple of hotels right on the beach, with The Inn (see page 109) being a particularly good choice for lunch. You can use their loungers and umbrellas if you eat there.

Pillars of Hercules

On the other side of Charlotte Point, which caps Galleon Beach to the west, the Pillars of Hercules are a section of cliff that has been strikingly eroded to form huge striated pillars of rock, some 20 m (66 ft) high. You can just about catch a glimpse of the Pillars from Fort Berkeley, and can walk around to them from Galleon Beach (wear shoes that you don't mind getting wet), but most people prefer to see them from the sea, which provides the best vantage point. Water-taxis at the Antigua Yacht Club Marina will be happy to oblige.

TAKING A BREAK

Shirley Heights Lookout ££ ❶   With a beautiful setting in a historic building overlooking English Harbour, this is a truly atmospheric spot, serving tasty local food, including seafood, chicken and steak, with specials chalked up on a blackboard. It's also a good spot for a sundowner, and, apart from Thursday and especially Sunday evenings, it is generally quiet. ⓐ Shirley Heights ❶ 460 1785 ⓦ www.shirleyheightslookout.com ❶ 09.00–22.00 Tues–Sun, 09.00–sunset Mon ❶ Admission charge Sun

◆ *Enjoy the stunning scenery at Galleon Bay*

Fig Tree Drive & the interior

With its relatively flat proportions and tiny dimensions, Antigua doesn't have the extensive rainforest of other islands. Its interior is covered in a lush canopy of tropical growth, but the majority of the land has been developed in some way – planted with bananas and other fruit and vegetables, or given over to cattle pastures. Nonetheless, the winding route of Fig Tree Drive, which loops inland between Carlisle Bay and Swetes, offers some very picturesque views over the interior, and makes a pleasant half-day excursion.

THINGS TO SEE & DO

Carlisle Bay and Old Road

Heading south along the island's west coast road, the route starts at Curtain Bluff. This is a tiny promontory that has a lovely undeveloped swathe of beach, backed by an extensive grove of palms, on one side, and another picture-perfect beach, lined with the buildings of the Curtain Bluff hotel, on the other side. Past the hotel, the route swings through the pretty little village of Old Road, birthplace of the footballer Emile Heskey, and then heads inland.

Fig Tree Drive

The roadside buildings become few and far between as you enter Fig Tree Drive, with plantations of bananas (the local name is figs) overhanging the tarmac and cows grazing in lush pastures. A little way up into the hills, the **Rainforest Canopy Tour** offers a fun way to get up close to the forest, with a system of nine zip-wires strung between the trees. Attached to the lines with a harness, you swing through the canopy at a height of around 100 m (350 ft) in some places – an exhilarating experience. There's also a wobbly suspension bridge to cross, various rope challenges to climb and short trails between the zip-wires. Note that participants need to be over four feet in height and over seven years old. Wear covered shoes and long trousers.

○ *Bunches of bananas along Fig Tree Drive*

🔺 *St Barnabas Church, Liberta*

Canopy Tour ⓐ Fig Tree Drive ⓣ 562 6363 ⓦ www.antiguarainforest.com
🕐 08.00–18.00 daily ⓘ Admission charge; age and height restrictions
apply

Swetes to Liberta

Fig Tree Drive ends at the village of Swetes, a nondescript sort of place
best known as the birthplace of two West Indies cricketers: fast bowler
Curtly Ambrose and wicketkeeper Ridley Jacobs, both now retired. Past
the huge Our Lady of Perpetual Help Catholic Church, turn right to get
to Liberta, one of the first Free Villages in Antigua established by former
slaves after emancipation. Characterised by its diminutive clapboard
homes, the village boasts a couple of beautiful churches, such as the
brick-built church of St Barnabas.

▶ *Admiral's Inn, Nelson's Dockyard*

Food & drink

LOCAL FOOD

Although Antigua is too small to grow all of the fruit and vegetables it requires (much of it is imported from Dominica), local cuisine is nonetheless delicious and makes excellent use of Caribbean produce, as well as imported foods such as saltfish, cooked up with onion, garlic and tomatoes as a delicious breakfast dish.

The national dish, pepperpot, is a spicy stew of salted pork and beef cooked with chicken, pigeon peas (a popular pulse), pumpkin, okra, aubergine and spinach. It's usually served with fungi, which is a thick dollop of boiled seasoned cornmeal, sometimes cooked with okra. Other specialities to look out for include *chop-up* or *chop-chop*, a delicious blend of chopped aubergine with okra and spinach; *bamboola*, a thick savoury bread made with cassava flour; and *ducunu*: grated sweet potato, coconut, spices and sugar, mixed with flour and milk and cooked in a banana-leaf wrapping. Look out also for the delicious local soups, such as fortifying pumpkin, and conch or goat water. Goat is also curried and served with white rice.

Antiguans have also become avid consumers of foods that originate on other Caribbean islands. Hailing from Trinidad, *roti* is a ubiquitous lunch snack, consisting of a flour wrap (a 'skin') folded over a mix of curried meat (sometimes conch, too) as well as vegetables, chickpeas and potato. You'll also see smoking roadside barbecues churning out jerk chicken, marinated in pimento and other spices and cooked over coals – spicy and delicious, and great after a few rums.

Seafood is uniformly delicious here. Barbudan lobster – much of the Eastern Caribbean imports its supply from here – is fantastic, either cooked with garlic butter, curried or spiced up in a tomato-based Creole sauce. As for varieties of fish, you'll see plenty of red snapper, a firm but light white fish, as well as meatier and sweet mahimahi or dorado. Shrimp are often curried in a coconut sauce, and you also see curried conch, the dense and delicious dweller of those beautiful pink shells sold on craft stalls. It's also made into fritters and, occasionally, served raw as a ceviche, marinated in lime and chopped up with peppers and onion. Other local seafood not to be missed includes cockles and whelks, usually steamed to perfection with garlic and herbs.

Most meals are accompanied by the staple side dish of 'rice and peas' (seasoned rice cooked with pigeon peas or kidney beans). You may also get ground provisions, the local name for hearty boiled tubers such as yam, dasheen, eddo and cassava. You'll also see potatoes in familiar forms: baked, mashed or served as chips. Other common side dishes include fried plantain, a few slices of creamy local avocado, coleslaw and green salad.

VEGETARIANS

There's usually a vegetarian option – often a tomato-based pasta dish – on most menus, and you could also ask for side dishes of stewed lentils or kidney beans to be served in main-course portions. Cheesy macaroni pie is also a tasty alternative. Look out, too, for Rastafarian Ital food shops, selling vegetarian or vegan food such as stewed tofu, soya chunks and various other veggie concoctions.

DESSERTS & FRUITS

Locally made ice cream, in flavours such as rum and raisin or coconut, is well worth trying. Tourist-oriented restaurants also have the full range of familiar desserts, from chocolate fudge cake to tiramisu. Fruits are a great way to finish a meal; the tiny Antiguan black pineapple – the island's national fruit – is very sweet and flavourful. Depending on the season, you'll also see fat and juicy mangoes, fragrant soursops encased in a green and prickly skin, and *pommeracs* – pear-shaped red fruits with a delicately scented white flesh. Bananas are always delicious, with many varieties to choose from – the mini finger bananas are especially sweet.

DRINKS

Soft drinks and bottled water are available everywhere; some unusual ones to try are *Malta*, a fortifying malt-based fizzy drink, and *Ting*, a refreshing grapefruit soda. You'll also sometimes see *Mauby*, a bittersweet drink flavoured with boiled-down tree bark. Other natural juices are also well worth seeking out, from tart tamarind and June-plum (also called golden apple) to passion fruit and guava. Perhaps the most refreshing drink of all is a freshly opened jelly coconut; vendors chop off the top with a machete to let you get at the sweet water, then cut the nut in half and chop off a bit of the shell for you to use to scoop out the soft white jelly.

As for alcohol, the local beer is *Wadadli*, a light and flavourful lager christened in honour of the Amerindian name for Antigua. You can also get Heineken and Jamaican Red Stripe, and other imports such as Carib, Corona and Grolsch. The basis of many a fruity cocktail, *Cavalier* rum is made at Antigua's distillery and comes in white, gold and overproof varieties. There's also a five-year-old and a 1981 vintage rum, both aged in oak casks. The same distillery also makes *English Harbour*, which again comes in white, gold and extra old varieties, the latter in a pretty gift box.

RESTAURANTS

Antigua's resorts – particularly Falmouth and English Harbour, Dickenson Bay, Jolly Bay and St John's – are home to a wide variety of restaurants, serving everything from Italian food to English-style pub grub or sushi. Of course, there are also countless places specialising in Caribbean cuisine. On that note, look out for mobile vans and small snackettes (cafés) knocking out inexpensive local food at lunchtime – a great way to sample Antiguan cuisine.

Few of the restaurants require smart dress, though you'll probably feel more comfortable in long trousers rather than shorts after dark. It's a good idea to book ahead, especially in high season. In low season, when many restaurants close down, it's sensible to ring ahead in any case to check that your restaurant of choice is open.

Cavalier rum is a local favourite

Shopping

Antigua offers some pretty decent shopping, with the Redcliffe Quay and Heritage Quay malls home to a huge array of stores, many of which sell duty-free goods, from jewellery to brand-name watches and clothing. Good-quality craftwork is available from the Vendors' Mall in St John's and from small shops island-wide, and there are also plenty of fine shops at the Woods Centre, on Friar's Hill Road, just north of St John's.

SUPERMARKETS

The best supermarkets on the island are the **Epicurean** at Jolly Harbour and the **Woods Centre**, both of them large and modern with a wide variety of local and imported produce, as well as a delicatessen selling cheese and cold meats. They also do decent takeaway snacks. The **Gourmet Basket** (in the Island Provision Complex on the George H Walter Highway – formerly Airport Road – close to V C Bird Airport) has a

⬤ *Colourful shopfronts brighten the experience*

great stock of speciality food and wine. Otherwise, there's **Bailey's** supermarket on the main road in Falmouth, and small stores selling basic items in every village. All these outlets have fresh produce, but you'll get the best selection if you head to the public market in St John's (see page 17), where the vendors can explain what everything is and tell you how to prepare it.

HERITAGE QUAY

With two floors of shops adjacent to the cruise ship dock in St John's, Heritage Quay is angled towards the tastes of cruise passengers. Alongside the shops selling jewellery and crystal figurines, stores to look out for include a branch of the UK's Body Shop, very convenient if you forget to stock up on your favourite products, as well as Beach Stuff and Sunseakers, both of which have a nice line in swimwear and associated beachwear, as well as caps, sunglasses and beach bags. Gingerlily sells lovely linen clothing, from capri trousers to maxi dresses, and the Music Shop has a good stock of reggae, soca and calypso CDs.

REDCLIFFE QUAY

The setting here is a lot more atmospheric than Heritage Quay, with shops set in the old cut-stone buildings. Island Woman has a stylish selection of clothing, bags and belts, while Rasta Pasta has a huge variety of quality craft items ranging from head-wraps to hammocks, not only from Antigua, but also from the rest of the Caribbean, Africa and Latin America. The Toy Shop, meanwhile, is an interesting little place crammed with toys and old-fashioned British sweets.

VENDORS' MALL

In between Redcliffe and St Mary's streets, the Vendors' Mall is a veritable Aladdin's cave of craftwork, with the rows of shops festooned with sarongs, t-shirts, hats, clothing and souvenirs – easily the largest selection of crafts on the island. Look out for wooden sculptures carved by local artists, beautifully decorated calabashes and jewellery made from Antiguan seeds, shells and stones.

Children

Antigua and Barbuda is a great destination for children. No vaccinations are needed, the water is safe to drink and standards of food hygiene are high, so there's no need to worry about stomach upsets from eating salads, ice cream and the like. The warm, calm waters of the Caribbean – not to mention the sandy beaches – are perfect for children, offering hours of play. Long Bay is an especially suitable spot, with very shallow water that is protected by a reef, but any of the west coast beaches are great for families.

You can buy buckets, spades and inflatables in Antigua, but it's sensible to use items such as lilos only in pools – it's possible to drift out to sea extremely quickly, even on a calm day.

BE SUN-SMART

As the tropical sun can be very strong, it's essential to protect your child's skin. Slather on the high-factor suncream, put them in t-shirts or custom-made UV-protective swimming gear when on the beach, and make sure they wear hats – those with flaps to protect the neck are especially good. Above all, make sure they don't play in the sun throughout the hottest part of the day (11.00–15.00) and keep them hydrated with lots of water.

ATTITUDES TOWARDS CHILDREN

Most people in Antigua and Barbuda love children and are very indulgent towards them, and travelling with youngsters will ensure you meet and interact with many more locals than you would in an adults-only group. However, bear in mind that, while children are cherished here, attitudes to parenting can seem quite old-fashioned compared to those in Europe or North America. Antiguan children are taught to be respectful of adults at all times, and backchat will certainly raise a few eyebrows, as will all-out tantrums. It's also sensible to follow the locals and put your children in trunks or swimming costumes whenever they

◓ *Playing in the sand at Dickenson Bay*

go to the beach – Antiguan children don't tend to swim naked. You may also find that older Antiguans are quite free with their advice on the correct way to look after your child – such as covering babies' heads (with a hat, for example) if they're out after dark.

ATTRACTIONS FOR CHILDREN

Although the beach is enough to keep many children absorbed for an entire holiday, there are plenty of other things for them to do.

Boat trips

The **Black Swan** 'pirate' ship (see opposite) is one of the most child-friendly options. They encourage children to dress up for their cruise, teach them 'pirate speak' and allow them to steer the vessel.

Horse riding and jeep safaris

These are two exciting and very different ways to see the island and are great for older children (see pages 100 and 102).

Mini-golf

In Dickenson Bay, the mini-golf course at Tattooz (see page 30) is great for children during the day, and there are other attractions in the area that, while not specifically designed for little ones, will usually keep them amused.

Watersports

Ultramarine (see page 98) offers duck diving, snorkelling and 'seafaris' for children.

EATING OUT

In tourist areas, children are welcomed in restaurants, many of which have children's menus, but you won't find local family parties dining out late as you would in, say, Spain or Italy, nor will you win over the staff if your children run rampant or scatter their toys between the tables.

Sports & activities

There are plenty of reasons to take time out from Antigua and Barbuda's beaches, with one of the main draws being the numerous watersports on offer. Head out onto the water to snorkel, scuba dive, kayak or swim with stingrays, or take a gentle cruise or exhilarating powerboat ride around the coast. On land, you can tour the island in an open-top jeep, go horse riding or swing through the forest canopy on a zip-wire, and then relax in a spa to recover from it all.

BOAT TOURS

There are several companies offering offshore cruises around Antigua and Barbuda. Many are aboard catamarans, which ride the waves smoothly and often have nets for sunbathing strung between the hulls. Most also offer an open bar and include lunch in the tour fee. Operated by **Tropical Adventures**, the *Excellence* is one of the biggest and fastest catamarans; it does a Barbuda trip (see page 66) as well as a circumnavigation of Antigua, with stops at Green Island (for swimming and snorkelling) and Nelson's Dockyard. **Wadadli Cats**, probably the largest operator, does pickups from many west coast beaches. They have a west coast cruise that includes snorkelling on Cades Reef and a swim at Turner's Beach; a Bird Island trip, which is especially good for children, with swimming and snorkelling in calm, shallow waters; and a circumnavigation of the island, with a stop at Green Island for swimming and lunch.

The *Black Swan*, a beautiful wooden schooner with the classic pirate ship proportions, offers a 'Pirate' cruise, with swimming at Deep Bay, lunch and an open bar, and a DJ who encourages dancing and walking of the plank. They also have sunset trips during which there is a greater emphasis on partying.

For something a little different, **Adventure Antigua** offer their 'Xtreme Circumnav', a *Miami Vice*-style high-speed zip around Antigua that packs in stops at Stingray City, Nelson's Dockyard, Green Island, the Pillars of Hercules and Rendezvous Bay. A more sedate option, their

Eco-Tour takes in the islands of the North Sound Marine Park. Guides give comprehensive information on the flora and fauna of the area, and there are stops at Great Bird Island (for a nature walk, swimming, snorkelling and lunch) and Hell's Gate near Devil's Bridge (for swimming). They also do a 'Classic Yacht' cruise, with snorkelling at Cades Reef, lunch at Carlisle Bay and the chance to try your hand at sailing the boat, built by hand in Carriacou.

Adventure Antigua ☎ 726 6355 Ⓦ www.adventureantigua.com
Black Swan ☎ 562 7946 Ⓦ www.piratesofantigua.com
Tropical Adventures ☎ 480 1225 Ⓦ www.tropicalad.com
Wadadli Cats ☎ 462 4792 Ⓦ www.wadadlicats.com

DIVING & SNORKELLING

Antigua and Barbuda offer some good diving and snorkelling, with the extensive Cades Reef off the southwest coast being home to some of the best coral and fish. There's also lots of interesting sea life just offshore of the Pillars of Hercules, around the islands of the North Sound Marine Park and around Mamora Bay. However, almost all of the beaches have some reef to explore within swimming distance of the shore, and, if you don't have your own snorkel and mask, you can rent gear from beach restaurants or dive shops. You can also buy equipment from AquaSports in Heritage Quay and Jolly Harbour. Most dive schools offer PADI certification courses as well as guided dives and snorkelling excursions. Ultramarine specialise in diving for children and also have hand-held 'seafari scooters' that motor you along on top of and below the water.

AquaSports ⓐ Heritage Quay ☎ 480 3090
ⓐ Jolly Harbour ☎ 480 3095 Ⓦ www.aquasportsantigua.com
Indigo Dive ⓐ Jolly Harbour ☎ 562 3483 Ⓦ www.indigo-divers.com
Jolly Dive ⓐ Jolly Harbour ☎ 462 8305 Ⓦ www.jollydive.com
Seawolf Diving School ⓐ Dockyard Drive, English Harbour ☎ 783 3466 Ⓦ www.seawolfdivingschool.com
Ultramarine ⓐ Sunsail Club Colonna, Hodges Bay & St James's Club, Mamora Bay ☎ 463 3483 Ⓦ www.ultramarinecaribbean.com

◒ Jump aboard a Wadadli Cats catamaran

FISHING

The waters around Antigua and Barbuda present rich pickings in terms of game fish such as marlin, tuna, wahoo, shark and barracuda. There are legions of sport fishing boats available for half- or full-day charters.

Antigua Fishing ☎ 463 3112 ⓦ www.antiguafishing.com
Phill's Eco Fishing ☎ 786 4347 ⓦ www.philsecofishing.com

GOLF

Antigua has two golf courses. The **Jolly Harbour Golf Club** has an 18-hole course adjacent to the marina and overlooking the ocean, and is open to non-members for a daily rate. They also offer weekly and monthly membership. Just outside St John's, **Cedar Valley** is another 18-hole course open to non-members, with green fees by the day or per week. You can rent clubs and buggies or take lessons at both courses.

Cedar Valley Golf Club ⓐ Cedar Valley ☎ 462 0161
ⓦ www.cedarvalleygolfag.com
Jolly Harbour Golf Club ⓐ Jolly Harbour Marina ☎ 462 7771 ext. 608

HELICOPTER TOURS

Caribbean Helicopters have two tours, which give an amazing bird's-eye view of Antigua and its reef-studded waters. The half-hour circumnavigation takes in the whole island, while the 20-minute half-island tour covers the southwest. They also do a 45-minute trip to volcano-ravaged Montserrat.

Caribbean Helicopters ⓐ Jolly Harbour ☎ 460 5900
ⓦ www.caribbeanhelicopters.com

HORSE RIDING

Spring Hill Riding Club, close to English Harbour, offers trail rides through the interior up to Fort George on Monk's Hill and down to the sea, with the chance to swim with your horse on Rendezvous Beach. They also provide riding lessons and more advanced showjumping and dressage tuition, and the horses are extremely well kept.

Spring Hill Riding Club ⓐ Falmouth ☎ 460 7787 or 773 3139

The Black Swan *at Dickenson Bay*

JEEP TOURS

Several companies do jeep tours of the island's main attractions, from English Harbour and Devil's Bridge to the North Sound Marine Park (see page 39) or Stingray City (see page 40). They also go off-road to Fort George on Monk's Hill and to secluded beaches. **Adventure Antigua** have a fleet of customised zebra-striped open-top jeeps, while **Happy Trails** have air-conditioned vehicles.

Adventure Antigua ☎ 726 6355 Ⓦ www.adventureantigua.com
Happy Trails ☎ 464 2089 Ⓦ www.happytrailsantigua.com

SPAS

Antigua has several spas offering a range of treatments. One of the best is the international-standard **Blue Spa** at the lovely **Carlisle Bay** hotel, with a sauna, plunge pools and treatment rooms. If you're after a massage, **Chakra Bodyworks** are an excellent choice, doing many different types of massage, be it Ayurvedic, deep tissue, shiatsu or reiki. They also offer yoga classes.

Blue Spa ⓐ Carlisle Bay ☎ 484 0025 Ⓦ www.carlisle-bay.com
Chakra Bodyworks ⓐ Jolly Harbour ☎ 772 6491
Ⓦ www.chakrabodyworks.com

Festivals & events

Antigua and Barbuda's biggest events revolve around sailing, with the Classic Yacht Regatta and Antigua Sailing Week, both usually in April, drawing the largest crowds. Otherwise, Carnival in July is a brilliant explosion of colour and music, and there are smaller-scale sporting events and regattas throughout the year. Note that dates for some of the events vary from year to year, so consult the tourist board website (see page 113) for confirmation.

FEBRUARY
Valentine's Day Regatta Two-day regatta held at the Jolly Harbour Yacht Club, with several short races and two classes of competing yachts. ⓐ Jolly Harbour Marina ⓣ 461 6300

MARCH
Antigua & Barbuda Culinary Festival Three days of cooking competitions, culinary seminars and a food fair to showcase the talents of local and international chefs. ⓐ Staged at various venues across Antigua ⓣ 728 3343 ⓦ www.antiguaculinaryfestival.com

APRIL
Antigua Classic Yacht Regatta One of the most prestigious classic yacht events in the world, this three-day regatta in the week preceding Sailing Week offers the chance to see some truly beautiful boats – including magnificent tall ships. Many are wooden schooners, but modern fibreglass boats also compete, and there are several good vantage points to view the races on Falmouth Harbour. The day before the regatta, the 50-plus competitors anchor at the Yacht Club Marina to be judged in the Boat International Concours d'Elegance competition, which sees them assessed for the best-maintained craft. In the Heritage Day festival after the last day of racing, crews dress up in period costume and a huge tea party is held at the Admiral's Inn in Nelson's Dockyard. ⓐ Antigua Yacht Club Marina ⓣ 460 1799 ⓦ www.antiguaclassics.com

◗ *Lively events will keep the whole family entertained*

Antigua Sailing Week Staged in Antigua since 1967, this is now one of the biggest events in the sailing calendar, with more than 200 boats taking part, and many more yachts of all shapes and sizes descending to soak up the scene and take part in the huge array of associated events. Marquees and food stalls are set up in the streets around Nelson's Dockyard and the Antigua Yacht Club Marina, and a carnival atmosphere takes over the island, making Sailing Week one of the best times of year to visit Antigua. Races start in Dickenson Bay and Falmouth Harbour, with the world's top boats competing to take the prestigious Lord Nelson Trophy. Other races include a 'Round Redonda Race' to Antigua and Barbuda's tiny uninhabited territory, a race to Guadeloupe and back, and a circumnavigation of the island for the Yachting World Trophy.
📞 462 8872 🌐 www.sailingweek.com

Back II Life Staged by the UK-based Soul II Soul sound system, this excellent event comprises a series of parties around the island during Sailing Week with music from renowned DJs Norman Jay, David Rodigan and Trevor Nelson. Many people attend as part of a package holiday, but you can also buy events-only tickets. 📞 020 7439 6060 (in UK) 🌐 www.soul2soul.co.uk/back2life

Mount Gay Rum Party Massive beach party sponsored by Barbados' number one rum, with giveaways and a huge crowd dancing on the sand. The entry fee covers food and drink. 📍 Pigeon Beach, Falmouth Harbour 📞 480 5180

MAY

Antigua and Barbuda Sport Fishing Tournament Well-attended event with lots of associated parties at Jolly Harbour and English Harbour.
📞 460 7400 🌐 www.antiguabarbudasportfishing.com

Sweet Cry Antigua Staged in the spectacular location of Dow's Hill, overlooking English Harbour and with panoramic views over the rest of the island, this is an excellent little music festival held on the last days of Sailing Week, showcasing some local and international reggae, soul, calypso and zouk acts. 🌐 www.sweetcryfreedom-antiguabarbuda.com

JUNE
Romantic Rhythms Music festival first staged in 2008, with two concerts at the Sir Vivian Richards Stadium and another on Fort Beach outside St James. ☎ 462 0480 ⓦ www.antiguamusicfestival.com

JULY & AUGUST
Antigua Carnival Ten days of classic Caribbean Carnival events, from calypso and steel band competitions to huge outdoor parties and the crowning of the Carnival Queen. Festivities culminate in the Monday and Tuesday parades of costumed bands through the streets of St John's. Before these two main parades, there's also a children's carnival, held in the Antigua Recreation Ground on the Sunday and there's Jouvert, the rather wild opener to Carnival, which starts from 04.00 on the Sunday night/Monday morning of the main parades, and sees revellers slinking through the streets coated in mud or body paint. Anyone can join a Jouvert or costume band. For details of bands and the registration process, visit the website ⓦ www.antiguacarnival.com

NOVEMBER
Independence Celebration of Antigua and Barbuda's independence from Britain on 1 November 1981 by way of parades and activities in and around St John's. The buildings throughout the capital are draped in the colours of the national flag. ☎ 562 1725 ⓦ www.independence.gov.ag

DECEMBER
Charter Yacht Show Primarily a trade show, but still a great chance to view what's new in the boating world, including some fantastically luxurious super-yachts. Boats moor at Nelson's Dockyard and at the Falmouth Harbour marinas. ☎ 460 1059 ⓦ www.antigua-charter-yacht-meeting.com

⏵ *The national flag flaps in the wind*

Accommodation

The prices below relate to the cost of sharing a double room in the high season. During the low season, rates can reduce by up to around 25 per cent. Most hotels will quote the rate in US$.

£ = US$70–160   **££** = US$161–250   **£££** = over US$250

Note that most hotels add an extra 10.5 per cent government tax and 10 per cent service charge to their rates.

EAST COAST

Grand Pineapple Beach Resort ££ Spreading back from the pristine sands of one of Antigua's best beaches, this hotel has clean, appealing rooms, decent restaurants offering local and international cuisine, and good facilities, including tennis courts, watersports and a fitness centre.
ⓐ Long Bay ⓣ 463 2006 ⓦ www.grandpineapple.com

St James's Club £££ A friendly place with comfortable and handsomely furnished rooms, located on two secluded beaches. The excellent facilities include several restaurants and bars, a spa, four pools, a kids' club and watersports. ⓐ Mamora Bay ⓣ 462 5000
ⓦ www.eliteislandresorts.com

FALMOUTH & ENGLISH HARBOUR

Antigua Yacht Club Marina ££–£££ Choose from one of the gorgeous self-contained studios overlooking Falmouth Harbour and the marina, or one of the rooms in the main building. All are stylish and beautifully finished. There's also a steam room, a sauna and an excellent restaurant.
ⓐ Falmouth Harbour ⓣ 562 3030 ⓦ www.aycmarina.com

The Inn £££ Classy place on the beach, with elegantly decorated rooms and a range of facilities, including a pool, tennis courts, watersports and a fitness centre. The hotel has two restaurants – a beachside bistro and a terrace restaurant, ideal for candlelit alfresco dining – and the food is superb at both. ⓐ Galleon Bay, English Harbour ⓣ 460 1014 ⓦ www.theinn.ag

FIVE ISLANDS

Coconut Beach £–££ This is a charming, small, adults-only hotel, popular with couples and honeymooners seeking a tranquil retreat. The rooms front onto a semi-private beach, and each has a balcony and hammock. There are two restaurants, a wellness cottage, a pool, good watersports and evening entertainment. ⓐ Yepton Beach ⓣ 462 3239 ⓦ www.coconutbeachclub.com

Hawksbill ££ Set along four gorgeous beaches, including the island's only clothing-optional one, with rooms scattered around landscaped tropical gardens and a decent range of facilities, including watersports and a wellness centre. This hotel operates a no-smoking policy in its rooms, lounges, bars and restaurants. ⓐ Hawksbill Beach ⓣ 462 0301 ⓦ www.rexresorts.com

THE NORTH

Halcyon Cove £ This cheerful and comfortable place offers a range of decent rooms (all non-smoking), beach loungers on Dickenson Bay, a pool and watersports. It has a cocktail lounge and the Warri Pier restaurant, which is over the bay and prides itself on its romantic setting and delicious food. ⓐ Dickenson Bay ⓣ 462 0256 ⓦ www.rexresorts.com

Siboney Beach Club ££ This welcoming, small hotel is set in pretty tropical gardens right on the beach. Its elegant and comfortable suites are equipped with a kitchenette, living area and balcony or patio. Facilities include a pool, which is hidden among the palms and flowers, hammocks slung between the trees, and the Coconut Grove restaurant, which specialises in Caribbean cuisine. ⓐ Dickenson Bay ⓣ 462 0806 ⓦ www.siboneybeachclub.com

Trade Winds ££ Idyllic hotel on a hill overlooking Dickenson Bay, set in landscaped gardens, with a pool and excellent restaurant, where you can dine alfresco with views of the Caribbean Sea below. The rooms are decorated in a cool, contemporary style, and the staff are professional and friendly. ⓐ Dickenson Bay ⓣ 462 1223 ⓦ www.twhantigua.com

Blue Waters £££ Classy resort in a secluded cove with verdant tropical gardens and its own white-sand beach adjacent to Hodges Bay. This luxurious hotel has a variety of different rooms, three restaurants, a spa, lots of activities (including things for children) and nightly entertainment. ⓐ Blue Waters Bay ⓣ 462 0290 ⓦ www.bluewaters.net

Sunsail Club Colonna £££ This busy hotel boasts some of the island's best watersports facilities. Most guests stay specifically to go sailing, but there's also windsurfing, kayaking, snorkelling and scuba diving. The hotel has an open-air restaurant and traditional Caribbean bar, a spa, a fitness centre and a kids' club. ⓐ Hodges Bay ⓣ 462 6263 ⓦ www.sunsail.co.uk/clubs/destinations

WEST COAST

Jolly Beach Resort & Spa £–££ This hotel set right on Jolly Beach has a large pool and comfortable rooms in low-rise blocks. There are five restaurants offering a variety of delicious food, and plenty of activities, including watersports, a kids' club, a fitness centre and spa, tennis courts and nightly entertainment. ⓐ Jolly Beach ⓣ 462 0061 ⓦ www.jollybeachresort.com

Carlisle Bay £££ Very classy hotel with an exclusive feel, set in a truly stunning beach location, backed by a forested hillside. It has chic and spacious rooms, two outstanding restaurants, a spa, a fitness centre, tennis courts and a kids' club. ⓐ Carlisle Bay, Old Road ⓣ 484 0000 ⓦ www.carlisle-bay.com

Cocobay £££ Upmarket and intensely romantic all-inclusive hotel, popular with honeymooners. It is surrounded by gorgeous beaches and home to one of the island's best restaurants. The 49 cottages are very private, and facilities are excellent. ⓐ Valley Church beach ⓣ 562 2400 ⓦ www.cocobayresort.com

Curtain Bluff £££ High-class, all-inclusive hotel, located on a thin finger of land with beaches on either side. Operated by the same owners for 45 years, it's a very friendly place, with excellent facilities including a spa, tennis courts, croquet lawn, putting green and all watersports. The food is superb, too. ⓐ Old Road ⓣ 462 8400 ⓦ www.curtainbluff.com

⬤ The pool at Jolly Beach Resort & Spa

Preparing to go

GETTING THERE

Antigua is well served with international flights. From the UK, **British Airways** (☎ 0844 493 0787 ⓦ www.ba.com) has daily flights to the island from Gatwick, while **Virgin Atlantic** (☎ 0870 380 2007 ⓦ www.virgin-atlantic.com) flies three times a week from Gatwick. From Heathrow and Manchester, **BMI** (☎ 0870 6070 555 ⓦ www.flybmi.com) has direct flights each Friday, and can also offer flight and accommodation deals. Booking a package deal combining flights and accommodation can work out cheaper than arranging these separately, although there's then less choice in terms of which hotel you stay in. **First Choice** (☎ 0871 200 779 ⓦ www.firstchoice.co.uk) offers flight and accommodation packages in a range of hotels, such as the all-inclusive Sandals properties on Dickenson Bay. All the major UK travel agents also offer package deals. Flying time from the UK is around eight hours.

Many people are aware that air travel emits CO_2, which contributes to climate change. You may be interested in the possibility of lessening the environmental impact of your flight through the charity **Climate Care**, which offsets your CO_2 by funding environmental projects around the world. Visit ⓦ www.jpmorganclimatecare.com

TRAVEL INSURANCE

Taking out travel insurance is strongly recommended. There are excellent deals to be had, ranging from short break to annual cover. However, many of the basic options exclude certain activities, and if you are planning to go scuba diving or snorkelling, ride a motorbike or engage in other pastimes deemed higher risk, then you will almost certainly need to pay a little extra.

TOURISM AUTHORITY

The **Antigua and Barbuda Tourist Board** has several international offices, which can provide information, brochures and maps of the islands before your trip. Their website (ⓦ www.antigua-barbuda.org) also has content on activities, accommodation and dining. On the island, you can get information from the **Tourism Hospitality Unit** (ⓐ Upstairs at 25 Heritage Quay, St John's).

Tourist offices overseas

Canada Antigua and Barbuda Department of Tourism and Trade ⓐ 60 St Claire Avenue East, Suite 304, Toronto, Ontario M4T 1N5 ⓣ 416 961 3085 ⓔ info@antigua-barbuda-ca.com

UK Antigua and Barbuda Tourist Office ⓐ 2nd Floor, 45 Crawford Place, London W1H 4LP ⓣ 020 7258 0070 ⓦ www.antigua-barbuda.com

US Antigua and Barbuda Tourist Office ⓐ 3 Dag Hammarskjold Plaza, 305 E 47th Street, 6A, New York, NY 10017 ⓣ 212 541 4117 or 888 268 4227 ⓔ info@antigua-barbuda.org

Antigua Department of Tourism and Trade ⓐ 25 SE Second Avenue, Suite 300, Miami, FL 33131 ⓣ 305 381 6762

BEFORE YOU LEAVE

No vaccinations are required for Antigua and Barbuda, though you should make sure you're up to date with standard vaccinations, such as tetanus. The island's pharmacies are fairly good, but it's worth bringing your own first-aid kit in case of minor cuts and bruises. Bear in mind that it's important to keep cuts dry in the heat to prevent infection, so spray-on dry antiseptic is better than creams. Bring along any prescription drugs you take regularly and a good supply of suncream. You can buy the latter locally, but you may not get the brand, factor or quality that you're used to. Whatever your complexion, start off with at least factor 30. You might also want to bring a sun hat. Other essentials include insect repellent, as well as trousers and long-sleeved tops to put on when the mosquitoes come out at dusk. In general, light garments in natural fabrics are best, but you might want to take along something smart for nights out or meals in upmarket restaurants. It is illegal to wear camouflage clothing in Antigua and Barbuda, so leave these items at home.

ENTRY FORMALITIES

Citizens of the UK and most European countries as well as the US, Canada, Australia and New Zealand (among others) do not need a visa to enter Antigua and Barbuda, but must present a valid passport and onward ticket on arrival.

In terms of customs restrictions, visitors are allowed to enter the country with 200 cigarettes, or 50 cigars, or half a pound of loose tobacco, and one litre of wine or spirits.

MONEY

Antigua and Barbuda's currency is the Eastern Caribbean dollar (abbreviated as EC$). You'll often see goods and services priced in US dollars, too, and you can use US dollars to make payments (though you'll get your change in EC$). Cash and traveller's cheques can be exchanged at banks, most of which are located in St John's (High Street). There are also banks at Woods Shopping Mall, V C Bird International Airport, Nelson's Dockyard and Jolly Harbour Marina. All of them have ATMs that accept foreign cards, but they dispense EC$ only. Most hotels and tourist-oriented restaurants and bars accept credit cards, and you can also get cash advances on credit cards at most ATMs.

CLIMATE

Antigua and Barbuda's tropical climate means temperatures in the mid-20s Celsius (mid-70s Fahrenheit) in the winter, and the high 20s/early 30s Celsius (mid-80s Fahrenheit) in the summer. Average annual rainfall is just 114 cm (45 in), making them the driest (and sunniest) of the Eastern Caribbean islands, although trade winds blowing in from the northeast provide some pleasant breezes. Humidity is generally low, but things can get a bit sticky in the hot summer months. The weather is at its best between November and April, when the nights are cooler and the sun less oppressively hot. The hurricane season lasts from June to November, though direct hits are very rare.

BAGGAGE ALLOWANCES

Most airlines will allow you to travel with two checked bags of 23 kg (50 lbs) each, and a single piece of hand luggage. Some allow a laptop bag or handbag as well. You can usually pay an excess charge for checked bags over 23 kg, but few airlines will accept pieces that weigh more than 32 kg (70 lbs) for health and safety reasons. Continuing restrictions on liquids in hand luggage mean that you can only carry liquids or gels in containers of under 100 ml, and all liquids must be separated from the rest of your luggage in a clear zip-lock bag. As baggage allowances change frequently, however, it's best to check with your airline before you travel.

During your stay

AIRPORTS

All flights to Antigua touch down at the V C Bird International Airport, in the midst of the snazzy Stanford cricket complex in the northeast of Antigua. There are taxis to meet each flight, and prices are fixed; at the official booth, you're assigned a driver and told the price. At the time of writing, the fare to Dickenson Bay, for example, is EC$42 (US$16). The airport has an ATM, car rental booths, a restaurant with wireless internet, and duty-free stores in the departures lounge. Bus services are infrequent, so it's far better to take a taxi or rent a car. If you have a long wait ahead of you before a flight, you might want to kill time by walking over to the Sticky Wicket bar and restaurant (see page 75) and having a meal or drink overlooking the cricket ground.

DEPARTURE TAX

All foreign nationals must pay a departure tax of EC$50 (US$20) when leaving the island. You pay at the booth just before the entrance to the departures lounge at V C Bird Airport.

COMMUNICATIONS
Telephones

There are Cable & Wireless phone booths in all but the smallest of Antigua's towns and villages, most of which accept phonecards, which you can buy from pharmacies, hotels and post offices. You can make international calls from the booths. Most hotels have in-room phones from which you can dial abroad direct, but bear in mind that you'll pay a premium for this. You should be able to roam with most tri-band mobile phones on the islands, but, if you plan to make a lot of calls, you might want to buy a local SIM card and top up your credit as you need it; international calls made this way are far less expensive than calling from hotels. The main service providers are **APUA** (with outlets opposite the Cathedral on Long Street in St John's, at AquaSports in Jolly Harbour and at the National Parks Authority office in English Harbour), **bmobile** (with shops in the Woods Centre, High and Long streets in St John's, and Jolly Harbour) and **Digicel** (Redcliffe Street in St John's).

TELEPHONING ANTIGUA & BARBUDA

The country code for Antigua and Barbuda is 268. To call the islands from the UK, dial 001 followed by 268 and the seven-digit number. To call from the US, dial 1 followed by 268 and the seven-digit number.

TELEPHONING ABROAD

To call the UK from Antigua and Barbuda, dial 011 followed by 44 for the UK, then the area code (minus the first zero) followed by the number.

To call the US from Antigua and Barbuda, dial 1 followed by the area code and number.

Postal services

The post is a bit hit-and-miss in terms of delivery times. There are post offices on High Street in St John's, close to the Heritage Quay shopping centre, at the airport, at the Woods Shopping Mall near St John's and at Nelson's Dockyard. All are open 08.15–12.00 & 13.00–16.00 Mon–Thur, 08.15–12.00 & 13.00–17.00 Fri, and 09.00–12.00 Sat. Stamps are available from post offices, hotel gift shops and pharmacies, and many hotels will post cards and letters for you. Otherwise, take them direct to an office. Postcards cost EC$0.90 to send to the UK and Europe, and EC$0.75 to the US and Canada.

Internet

There are internet cafés with terminals and fast connections in all of the tourist centres; many hotels, restaurants and bars also have wireless networks. Some places charge for wireless access, but most have open networks that you can access for free.

CUSTOMS

Although Antigua and Barbuda can come across as a laid-back place, it is actually quite conservative, with the majority of the population being practising Christians. The locals certainly know how to have a good time, but public drunkenness and lewd behaviour are frowned upon. It is customary to greet people with a 'good morning/afternoon' when entering a shop or office; launch straight into a request without preceding it with the appropriate greeting and you'll be considered rude – and service may be slow or unhelpful as a result.

DRESS CODES

Given the tropical climate, it makes sense to choose clothing that will keep you cool and provide protection from the sun's rays. It's best to wear something that covers shoulders and arms, and it's advisable to don a hat. There are no specific customs for visiting churches, but wearing something relatively modest will be appreciated.

When it comes to swimwear, it's not a good idea to wear a swimming costume or bikini anywhere but the beach. To avoid causing offence, cover up properly or change into regular clothes before you venture away from the sand. Topless or nude sunbathing is illegal in Antigua and Barbuda, so on most beaches you should keep your clothes on. However, many hotels sit on what feel like 'private' strips of sand where many tourists do go topless, and one hotel, the Hawksbill (see page 109), has a clothing-optional beach. The best plan is to ask around and assess the scene before stripping off.

If you plan on going out clubbing, bring smart clothes. Antiguans dress up to the nines when they go out – though leave the killer heels at home if you're heading to Shirley Heights, as the cobblestone floor isn't very forgiving.

ELECTRICITY

Electric current is usually 10 volts, 60 cycles AC, with two-pin round or flat sockets. However, you'll also find 220 volts, 50 cycles AC and UK-style three-pin sockets in some hotels. It's best to bring a converter plug just in case. Hotels usually have these, but supplies may be limited.

EMERGENCIES

> ### EMERGENCY PHONE NUMBERS
> The police, fire department and ambulance service can all be reached on ☎ 999, ☎ 911 ☎ 562 2433. The main police station is in St John's. @ Newgate Street ☎ 462 0045.

If you are the victim of a crime, call the police on the above numbers, but bear in mind that the police service is underfunded and response times can be slow. You can also contact the consular representative of your home country:

British Consular Agent ☎ 764 4653
US Consular Agent ☎ 463 6531
French Consulate ☎ 460 6428
German Consulate ☎ 462 3174
Italian Consulate ☎ 460 1543

There are two hospitals in Antigua: the public **Holberton Hospital** (@ Queen Elizabeth Highway, St John's ☎ 462 0251), which has an A&E department, and the private **Adelin Clinic** (@ Fort Road, St John's ☎ 462 0866/7), which also has a casualty department and is a little nicer than Holberton. All hotels will be able to recommend a dentist or doctor in the event of minor ailments.

GETTING AROUND

By far the best way to get around is to rent a car, which is well worth the rental price if you plan to explore the island and make more than one or two evening excursions for dinner. However, taxis are widely available and there is a public bus system, albeit limited.

Car rental

There are legions of companies offering car rental in Antigua and, to a far lesser extent, Barbuda. Most offer regular cars and more rugged jeeps or 4×4 vehicles, which are great for coping with the often rough and potholed roads. To drive in the country you must purchase a temporary local driver's licence for EC$50 (US$20). All rental companies can organise these for you, and it will be valid for six months. In terms of the rules of the road, you should drive on the left, and the speed limit is 40 mph (64 km/h), though you'll find that local drivers will exceed this wherever there's a decent stretch of road. There are a few of these, especially around St John's and the airport, but don't expect three lanes and hard shoulders on the 'highways', which are generally indistinguishable from main roads.

Signage is pretty poor, but distances are so small that with the aid of one of the free road maps available throughout the island you should be able to navigate around – you can always stop and ask someone if in doubt. Look out for potholes, especially after dark, and animals on the road – you'll often have to slow down or stop to allow a herd of goats or a few cows to pass, and some will be trailing long tether ropes, which you should not drive over if at all possible. In general, it's important to drive defensively and be aware of other drivers doing things such as overtaking on corners. If you're travelling with children, don't rely on your car rental company to supply a car seat – bring your own from home.

Taxis

There are plenty of taxis in Antigua, distinguishable from private vehicles by their 'TX' plates. Many drivers tout for fares in busy areas such as Dickenson Bay or English Harbour, but in quieter districts you'll need to phone ahead and book a driver. All hotels can do this for you. Fares are set and most drivers carry an official price list with them, but make sure you agree on the price, and determine if it's in EC or US dollars.

Public transport

Antigua's bus service covers a number of routes, with services running from St John's to Dickenson Bay and the airport, the west coast, English Harbour, and Parham and Willikies on the east coast. Services to the east leave from the East Bus Terminus, close to the Antigua Recreation Ground, and those for the west from the West Bus Station, near the market. From the same terminuses, privately owned minibuses also cover most points on the island. Bear in mind, though, that services are infrequent and stop entirely after around 20.00, and that buses and minibuses don't leave until they are full. Most are not air-conditioned. Fares are, however, extremely inexpensive.

HEALTH, SAFETY & CRIME

Travel to Antigua and Barbuda doesn't pose any particular health risks. No vaccinations are required (though its advisable to be up to date with your tetanus vaccination). The water is chlorinated and drinkable, but most people stick to bottled water just to be on the safe side. Standards of food hygiene are generally excellent, so there's no reason to avoid salads, fruits, ice in drinks, ice cream and so on. The main thing to be careful of is the tropical sun, which can be fierce during the heat of the day, and which can burn even when it's cloudy. Limit time in the sun to 20-minute bouts between 11.00 and 15.00 when the rays are at their strongest, and always use high-factor suncream. Bear in mind also that it's especially easy to burn if you're out on the ocean, as the sun reflects off the water and the sea breezes mean you don't notice the heat. It's important to drink plenty of water – ideally two litres a day – to keep yourself hydrated and to ward off heatstroke.

Beware of spiny black sea urchins when snorkelling or diving, or walking over oceanside rocks; if you step on one, the thin spines can break off painfully in your foot and you should seek medical attention and douse the area in vinegar (or even urine at a push!). Be aware that there are a few manchineel trees growing close to beaches, identifiable by their flat, rounded leaves and green fruits that resemble a miniature apple. The fruits are extremely poisonous, as is the sap of the tree, so don't sit under one during rain, as the runoff from the tree will cause blistering of the skin and in some cases temporary blindness.

More of an annoyance than a health risk, mosquitoes can become quite a bother on Antigua and Barbuda. They are most prevalent at daybreak and dusk. You can buy repellent locally, but it's a good idea to bring some with you so that you can use it as soon as you arrive. Other sensible precautions include wearing long sleeves and trousers in the evenings, closing windows and patio doors before dusk, and sleeping under a net. Note that fans and air conditioning are great deterrents.

So far as healthcare is concerned, your hotel will be able to recommend a doctor on call, and anything more serious can be treated at Antigua's public or private hospitals (see page 119). The public hospital is poorly equipped in comparison to those in the UK or US, but standards of care are good. However, you may find the private clinic a better option, with less waiting time. It's important to take out a travel insurance policy that covers you for evacuation in the unlikely event of your becoming seriously ill, and, if you do get private treatment, make sure you obtain a receipt if you plan to claim back the money. Most of the island's pharmacies are in St John's, where the Ceco Pharmacy on High Street is open daily from 08.15 to 24.00. There are also pharmacies in the Woods Centre and at Jolly Harbour, though none in Falmouth or English Harbour.

Although Antigua made international headlines in 2008 following the tragic murder of two British tourists, crime levels are generally relatively low. Most of the incidents that do occur are drug-related. You should always take the common-sense precautions you would in any new place, and don't assume that the laid-back atmosphere means you can be lax about security. Don't carry large amounts of cash or wear expensive jewellery or watches, and always store valuables in hotel safes or deposit boxes. Avoid walking alone in isolated, unlit areas at night, and keep your wits about you when exploring St John's, where pickpocketing is not unknown. Make sure your accommodation is secure, with good locks on the windows and doors, and always lock up at night and when you go out. Keep car doors locked and don't leave valuables in your vehicle.

If you are unlucky enough to be the victim of a crime, it's essential to make a police report; if your property has been stolen, you must have a report in order to make an insurance claim. Antiguan police are not the most efficient in the world, but they are generally helpful and courteous. The police are easily recognisable by their grey shirts and dark trousers with a white stripe. Senior officers wear a khaki uniform.

Marijuana (*ganja* in Antigua) and cocaine are illegal here and penalties for possession and trafficking are severe.

MEDIA

Antigua and Barbuda has two daily papers, the *Sun* (🆆 www.antiguasun.com) and the *Observer* (🆆 www.antiguaobserver.com), with local news, sports and entertainment and coverage of Caribbean and international affairs. The local TV station, ABN (Antigua Broadcasting Network), shows mostly reruns of imported shows, as well as news and weather daily at 19.00. Most hotels and villas also have cable TV, showing mostly US entertainment channels, CNN, Fox News, BBC World News and BBC America, which carries some British programming. Observer Radio (91.1 FM) broadcasts a mix of phone-in shows and current affairs programmes, while ABN Radio (90.3 FM) is the island's official radio station. The BBC World Service is available on 89.1 FM.

OPENING HOURS

Opening hours for shops and businesses are generally 08.00–12.00 and 13.00–17.00 Monday–Saturday. Some shops close at 12.00 on Thursdays, and many in Heritage and Redcliffe quays open on Sundays, especially if there's a cruise ship in port. Most banks open 09.00–15.00 Monday–Thursday and 09.00–16.00 Friday. The market in St John's is open between around 06.00 and 17.00 Monday–Saturday.

RELIGION

The majority of the population of Antigua and Barbuda are practising Christians, and there are churches for several different denominations all over the islands. Modest attire is considered the norm for those entering places of worship.

SMOKING LAWS

There are no laws pertaining to smoking in Antigua and Barbuda, and it's fine to light up in most restaurants, bars and clubs (though other customers might not thank you for it). Some indoor, air-conditioned places allow smoking only in an outdoor area.

TIME DIFFERENCES

Antigua operates on Atlantic Standard Time, which is four hours behind the UK's Greenwich Mean Time and one hour ahead of Eastern Standard Time in the US.

TIPPING

It's customary to tip waiters between 10 and 15 per cent, though a service charge is automatically added to most bills. It's also usual to tip taxi drivers, and bellboys who help with luggage in hotels. You might also want to leave a tip for your chambermaid at the end of your stay.

TOILETS

Public toilets are pretty much non-existent in Antigua and Barbuda. Your best option is to head for a tourist-oriented restaurant or bar, or an international fast-food joint, where facilities are likely to be clean and serviceable.

TRAVELLERS WITH DISABILITIES

There's not much provision for travellers with disabilities in Antigua and Barbuda. Although the newer hotels have made themselves accessible for wheelchairs, with ramps and specially fitted bathrooms, the island can be a challenge in terms of getting around. Pavements – where they exist – often have high kerbs, and surfaces tend to be very uneven. Access to buses can also be pretty much impossible for wheelchair users. While awareness of disability issues is not that high here, you will generally find that people are more than willing to help you. For local support and information, contact the **Antigua and Barbuda Association of Persons with Disabilities** ⓐ PO Box W123, Woods Centre, St John's ⓣ 453 1539 ⓦ www.abapd.org. International organisations and companies offering travel advice and trips for people with disabilities include **Disability Travel (UK)** (ⓣ 020 7731 2111 ⓦ www.disabilitytravel.co.uk) and **Accessible Journeys (US)** (ⓣ 610 521 0339 ⓦ www.disabilitytravel.com).

ACKNOWLEDGEMENTS

The publishers would like to thank the following individuals and organisations for providing their copyright photographs for this book:

Trevor Double page 53
FOTOSEEKER.COM WinterPark Photography page 111
Dexter Lewis pages 1, 9, 13, 31, 41, 54, 58, 62, 67, 69, 76, 81, 83, 85, 86, 87, 91, 92, 95, 99, 101, 107
Polly Thomas pages 5, 10–11, 16, 18, 23, 27, 29, 36, 38, 40, 46, 48, 50, 60, 71, 74, 104

Project editor: Frances Darby
Typesetter: Donna Pedley
Proofreader: Ian Faulkner
Indexer: Marie Lorimer

Send your thoughts to
books@thomascook.com

- Found a beach bar, peaceful stretch of sand or must-see sight that we don't feature?
- Like to tip us off about any information that needs a little updating?
- Want to tell us what you love about this handy little guidebook and more importantly how we can make it even handier?

Then here's your chance to tell all! Send us ideas, discoveries and recommendations today and then look out for your valuable input in the next edition of this title.

Send an email to the above address or write to:
HotSpots Series Editor, Thomas Cook Publishing,
Thomas Cook Business Park, PO Box 227, Coningsby Road,
Peterborough PE3 8SB, UK